TORQUE FOR TEENS

MICHAEL DUGGAN

THOMSON

COURSE TECHNOLOGY

Professional ■ Technical ■ Reference

JUL 2008
W 1

ISBN-10: 1-59863-409-7
ISBN-13: 978-1-59863-409-9
Library of Congress Catalog Card Number: 2007906511
Printed in the United States of America
08 09 10 11 12 TW 10 9 8 7 6 5 4 3 2 1

Thomson Course Technology PTR,
a division of Thomson Learning Inc.
25 Thomson Place
Boston, MA 02210
http://www.courseptr.com

Publisher and General Manager, Thomson Course Technology PTR:
Stacy L. Hiquet

Associate Director of Marketing:
Sarah O'Donnell

Manager of Editorial Services:
Heather Talbot

Marketing Manager:
Mark Hughes

Senior Acquisitions Editor:
Emi Smith

Project Editor and Copy Editor:
Kim Benbow

Technical Reviewer:
Brad Strong

Teen Reviewer:
Parker Hiquet

PTR Editorial Services Coordinator:
Erin Johnson

Interior Layout Tech:
ICC Macmillan Inc.

Cover Designer:
Mike Tanamachi

CD-ROM Producer:
Brandon Penticuff

Indexer:
Sharon Hilgenberg

Proofreader:
Sara Gullion

To my incredibly patient mate, who puts up with my gaming babble even when her eyes are glazing over.

ACKNOWLEDGMENTS

First I want to thank my immediate family, friends, and co-workers, for their support. Thanks to Emi Smith, Kim Benbow, Brad Strong, and the rest of the team at Course Technology for such a terrific job. Thanks to GarageGames for the versatile and awesome game engine and community they've built. Thanks to Christophe Canon, Benjamin "Djaggernaut" Chavigner, Nermin, Manuel Marino, Josiah Pisciotta, Stephane Conde, Dylan Romero, Brett Seyler, Randel Reiss, Mark Frohnmayer, Tony Ramos, Ian Hardingham, Paul Taylor, and everyone else who helped this volume grow through your contributions! I couldn't have made it happen without you all.

ABOUT THE AUTHOR

Michael Duggan is the author of *The Official Guide to 3D GameStudio* (Course Technology, 2007) and runs GameMD.net, an online forum for game designers. He is primarily an artist and writer and has taught 3D animation and game design at North Arkansas College for the past three years. He also contributed to the foundations of the Gaming and Robotics curriculum at the fast-paced Bryan College based out of Kansas City. He is currently working on another book titled *Web Comics for Teens*.

Contents

INTRODUCTION

Welcome to *Torque for Teens!* Whether you're looking forward to becoming a designer in the game industry or just wanting to explore the software and show off your creations to your friends, this book will help you learn about a powerful 3D computer game engine and the techniques it takes to make your game ideas come to life.

This book is written in a tutorial format so that, as you read, you don't just process information but put it to immediate use and get hands-on learning to reinforce the knowledge. Through this book, you will start by creating a first-person shooter game called *Abandon All Hope;* but I hope that you will use the skills you learn with it to springboard your talents into making dozens of other computer games. If you find that you love to make games, you can consider it as a career goal and someday find yourself working in a company building the next *Halo* or *World of Warcraft*.

What You Will Learn from This Book

In *Torque for Teens,* you'll learn about the game industry, the process by which your favorite video games are made, and how to make your very own computer games using the Torque Game Engine from GarageGames. Torque is a fantastic tool for creating many genres of games, but it is vast and complex and, therefore, can appear somewhat daunting at first; but *Torque for Teens* will break it down for you with easy-to-understand techniques and make creating games with Torque a cinch.

Who Should Read This Book

Anyone who is interested in working in the game industry, who likes playing video games and would like to make their own, or someone who is interested in making games as a hobby and doesn't know where to start will find the contents of this book useful. The following chapters go over the specifics of creating games with the Torque Game Engine, but they also cover the very real day-to-day responsibilities game developers have to deal with. As this book is about designing computer games, you should have some experience with computers beforehand.

How to Use This Book

Each chapter first details generic and academic information about the subjects. This information is followed up by hands-on practice, and then completed with a summary of the steps learned. Each chapter will in some way further the achievement of an entire game assignment, which is the creation of *Abandon All Hope,* a first-person shooter game. Beginning with creating the terrain of Ravenscroft, a medieval island village, the homes and church upon the island, and the player character model, you will learn, step by step, the best techniques for completing a game in the Torque Game Engine.

How This Book Is Organized

Here are some specifics about the chapter breakdown for this book.

Chapter 1: So You Want to Be a Game Designer?—Before delving into game production, this introductory chapter will give you a quick run-down on the industry and how the development pipeline works.

Chapter 2: The Torque Game Engine—This chapter delves into the technical information behind the powerful Torque Game Engine, the history of GarageGames, and the other Torque versions.

Chapter 3: Creating a Basic Game Outline—Before beginning your game project, it is important to learn about planning, and thus about game outlines.

Chapter 4: Opening Your Garage—In this project chapter, you'll learn to start a new game design in Torque.

Chapter 5: Wide Open Spaces—This is the project chapter where you learn about the Terrain Editor and make the village of Ravenscroft.

Chapter 6: Interior Design Isn't for Interior Decorators—This chapter delves into the Torque Constructor application and how to make interiors for your project.

Chapter 7: This Isn't the Runway: Modeling 101—In this project chapter, you'll model and animate Little Reaper, the player avatar.

Chapter 8: Getting Gooey (GUI)—This chapter covers creating interfaces for games, and you'll create the menu screen for *Abandon All Hope*.

Chapter 9: The Sound and the Fury—This chapter delves into the intricacies of sound recording, sound engineering, voice direction, and the placing of sound effects in games.

Chapter 10: Me Game, You Mission—Finally, you'll learn how to program game features in TorqueScript.

Chapter 11: Multiplayer Setup—In this chapter, I discuss the matters of creating online games called MMOs and how TorqueNet makes it happen.

Chapter 12: Put Your Game Through the Test—This rather short chapter details bug reporting and fixing mistakes in your games.

Chapter 13: Designing Other Games—This chapter discourses on the designing of other games beyond the project in this book.

Chapter 14: Get the Word Out: Play This Game!—For the final chapter, I cover the advertisement of your games and setting up a MySpace account.

Appendix A: Web Resources—The first appendix has Web links to further online resources.

Appendix B: Tool Kits Reference—This appendix gives you the specifics of the content on the companion CD-ROM.

The Companion CD-ROM—I've stocked the companion CD for this book with files for use with the projects, as well as tools and resources for completing games (and demos of various games) that have been made with Torque.

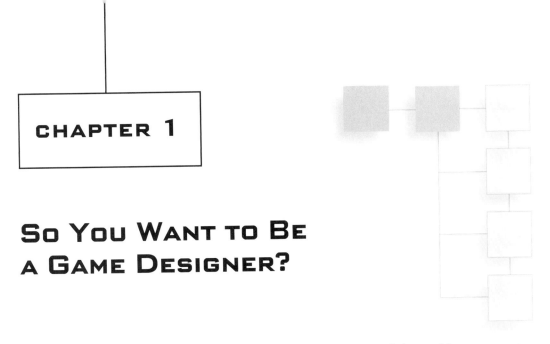

CHAPTER 1

So You Want to Be a Game Designer?

If you've picked up this book, you're probably interested in making computer games. You almost certainly have played these games before. You know what would make a great game and what would not. You might even have had a cherished nugget of an idea for a game you'd like to make rolling around in the back of your mind. I'll show you how to make your very own games through a step-by-step process. Along the way, you will gain further understanding of the principles behind game development.

By reading this book, you will learn how to make your own video games using the popular Torque Game Engine, one of the most affordable and multi-featured game engines on the market today. You will also learn whether you have what it takes to enter the exciting and multibillion-dollar industry of game design.

What a Game Designer Is and Is Not

Game design uses cutting-edge computer technology to create electronic games for the masses. Electronic games (which sprung up in the early 1960s) are making more than 11 billion dollars in the United States alone per year right now, and sales of video games have topped sales of CDs, videos, and DVDs—making more money than either the movie or music industry. This global expansion has ushered in a need for skilled programmers and talented game artists. Game design schools have sprung up all across the world in order to meet the rising demand for game development.

A single game may take a team of forty to ninety individual programmers, artists, animators, sound engineers, and directors—and may cost upwards of $500,000 to make. A game design team is often funded by a game publisher, such as Microsoft, Nintendo, or Electronic Arts, for exclusive publishing rights. Once the game is made, it must hit the store shelves running and make as much money in the first month as possible or it might wind up in the bargain bins or (gasp!) returned to the manufacturer.

Game designers fall into several classes (or categories) based on skill sets and specializations. The broadest classes of game designers are

- **Programmers**—These guys make the most money because they have to program the code that tells the computer what to do and how to react to the players playing the game.

- **Artists**—The work these guys do is the most readily apparent whenever you play a video game; they create the game's assets, including its environments, characters, props, weapons, vehicles, monsters, and more.

- **Writers**—Not only are these guys responsible for writing the story line behind the game, they also script the dialogue and events that take place in the game, as well as writing the game manual.

- **Sound Engineers**—The engineers set up the sound effects, compose the music mixes, and make the games sound so sweet.

- **Leaders**—The leaders communicate between the rest of the team, making sure that everyone is doing what they should and that the game development deadlines are reached.

Each of these game designer's roles can be further broken down by their special skill sets. Just to give you a short example, the game artists can include 2D texture artists, 3D model artists, 3D animators, riggers, sprite animators, interface artists, UV map artists, storyboard artists, animatic artists, motion graphics specialists, Web designers, and more.

Skill sets are very important within a game design team. In fact, if you graduate from a game school, the majority of employers will judge you not on the classes you took in school but by your skills in computers or art. So if you want to get a job in the industry as a 3D animator, you have to show an employer what software programs you know really well (whether you know Maya, Max, Softimage, or another 3D program)—and you will have to show a portfolio of original artwork you've personally created. An employer may also want to see a demo reel of any animations you have made yourself. A preferred bonus to recruiters will be if you can show them a game you have already completed!

That is why it is so important for you—right now—to start making computer games. You want to show not only your friends and relatives but the whole world that you have what it takes to be a game designer right this very moment. The beauty of the Torque Game Engine is that you do not have to be a computer genius to get started. You can make great games without hiring a whole game design team or spending $500,000. You can make games all by yourself!

What About Independent Game Design?

The music industry has existed for a lot longer than the game industry, and as anyone who knows music can tell you, the Top 40 pop music lists are fine for most listeners, but if you want to really hear some edgy tunes that take tired formulas for a ride on the wild side, indie music is where it's at!

Indie musicians are artists who aren't afraid to take risks. They will settle for smaller gigs and less pay if they can play the music they want to and experiment with their sonic art. Indie musicians are often seen as rebels who thumb their noses at the big industry giants.

Games work precisely the same way. When a corporate giant such as Electronic Arts pours millions of dollars into creating a big-market game, they expect huge payoffs to compensate for their costs. They are understandably against taking any sort of risks, even if the payoff might come in better innovation or storytelling. This undeniable fact is why you see so many game sequels and imitation knockoffs instead of seeing original or ground-breaking games on store shelves.

If you want to see real innovation in the game industry, you have to peer at the margins, at the indie game designers. Greg Costikyan (see Figure 1.1) coined the term "scratchware" (meaning a game created on the cheap) when he scripted

Figure 1.1
Greg Costikyan of Manifesto Games (image courtesy of Ellie Lang, 2006).

the Scratchware Manifesto, which called for game designers to stop paying attention to last year's A-lists and start developing novel game experiences. He has now taken a stand as an indie game publisher at Manifesto Games.

Scratchware and indie games are often shorter, cheaper-made games, developed by less than 10 people, and are free or sell low-priced over the Internet. Just giving away your game doesn't sound very smart, and when you see prices at $10 a purchase, it makes you wonder if indie developers ever make their money back—but it's been proven that even developers of the lowest-priced games can sell 4,000 copies in their first year. At $10 a pop, that comes to $40,000 in gross profits! Not bad for a part-time hobby, eh?

The indie game movement grew out of the Mod (short for modification) community, where players of popular games such as *Quake* and *Unreal* began modifying the components to build their very own game experiences and swap them online. Now supercharged with cheaper game engine licenses, a growing number of schools teaching game design, in addition to cheaper hardware and the emergence of indie game festivals where designers share tips and tricks, just about anyone can get in on the ground floor as an indie game designer!

As an indie developer, you can make any game you want. Because you're not taking anyone else's money to make your game, you can thumb your nose at tired conceptions and try radical things no one else has tried before. This book and the software with it give you all the tools you need to make your own computer games.

Tip

There is a great online community for gamers, developers, and publishers, and it should be your first stop when you are ready to advertise your homemade game. It is called the Great Games Experiment (or GGE) and was created by Jeff Tunnel, one of the founders of GarageGames. It has built-in widgets, forums, groups, and places to upload and play games of all kinds. A lot of first-time game developers go there to get their work noticed, so you ought to check it out. You can find it on the Web at www.greatgamesexperiment.com.

Game Design Step by Step

There are many levels, or steps, to designing killer games that you probably aren't even aware of. When you play a game, you don't see the years of sweat and hard work it took to polish that game into the fine piece of electronic make-believe you sit down to play. Though there are many steps taken to getting that game into your hands, the process can easily be broken down into three categories: pre-production, production, and post-production.

Pre-Production

The pre-production stage of game design is where the concept is created and finalized, funds are sought, and a team is put together to produce the game. The game design document is written, a game proposal or short demo may be shopped around to publishers, and a general inventory takes place before the designers ever get started.

Concept Creation

That killer game concept has to come from somewhere. A board meeting might brainstorm ideas until one or two trickle together that show merits of profit-making potential. A bunch of guys sitting around eating pizza may be joking about what games they would like to see and suddenly one of them says, "That's it!" Or one game designer may be taking a break from it all, enjoying a hot shower at home, and suddenly jumps out and grabs a notepad because a great idea has hit him. Whatever the concept is or looks like, it has sparked the development process.

Concept Finalization

The core team of the game's creators, often starting with the lead game designer, starts fleshing out the game. The artists come up with concept artwork, including drawings and paintings of the characters, vehicles, environments, and weapons that may be used in the game (see Figure 1.2). The writers come up with a game design document, which tells the team all the details of the game, including what levels there will be, who will be the characters in it, and how the player controls will work. The asset artists and programmers begin hashing together a short playable demo—what is often referred to as a *prototype*. The lead game designer works with his team to prepare a game proposal that is sure to knock the socks off of prospective backers.

Figure 1.2
Concept art used for *Darkwatch* (image courtesy of High Moon Studios, 2003).

Preparation

The team takes inventory of what software and hardware they have to start with, whether they have the office space needed to produce in, and how many members of the team they need to add by either hiring or outsourcing. This inventory helps shape their list of needed funds. Once they have the needed funds, they can get the help or tools necessary to produce the game.

Production

The team is now ready to begin game development in earnest. The asset artists (see Figure 1.3) design 3D models, 2D artwork, textures, and environments on their computers. The programmers code the player controls and character behaviors, as well as the physics engine. The writers set out dialogue and scripted events. The cinematic artists create short CG (computer graphics) cut-scenes that will appear throughout the game. And the leaders will make sure the office doesn't burn down and that the team members don't walk off the job. The production process often starts off dreamy and becomes more tense the closer deadlines get. Team members will often work obscene hours during the "crunch" time, even sleeping underneath their desks and avoiding their families.

Figure 1.3
A work station at High Moon Studios (image courtesy of High Moon Studios, 2007).

Post-Production

After the game is finished, it is still not finished. Testing, quality assurance, and bug-fixing commences, followed up by a PR (public relations) scheme that will market the game to its target audience. Even after the game is released and sitting on store shelves, more bug fixes may be required in the form of patch software.

Testing and QA

Testing involves the team members who are finished with the earlier tasks of playing the game over and over, carefully following checklists to make sure every possible glitch is rooted out. After the team tests their game, they may pull in people not related to the team to test the game with fresh eyes (see Figure 1.4). A beta version of the game may even be released online, requesting players to tell the team if a bug is discovered or offering prizes if players discover any glitch.

Quality assurance, or QA, is not really the same as testing. Team leaders are responsible, primarily guided by the project manager or head game designer, for

Figure 1.4
A test lab and observation deck for focus group testing (image courtesy of High Moon Studios, 2007).

making doubly sure that the game's overall look and playability remain consistent with the original concept. It can often happen that while 40 or so designers are working on a single project, some of them will start jumping off on tangents or try to change the look of the game part of the way through the build. So it's imperative that QA is maintained at every stage of production, especially during post-production.

Marketing

The game has to fly off store shelves within just a few weeks of getting there, so the PR department of a game developer or publishing company must make sure people know about the game before its release and that the target audience wants to buy it. Game magazines will feature previews of early prototypes of the game or interviews with its developers. Web forums are also a great place to hit the target audience. Any way that the PR people can whet the appetite of the public and make folks curious about an upcoming game is a good way to advertise it long before its release.

Expansion

Although the designers never intend for bugs to happen, the game may need patches to fix bugs that still occur in the product after it's shipped. The game may also prove wildly successful, and the developer may want to start work on expansion packs or sequels. If not, the game design team might get a moment to take a few breaths before starting their next new game project.

What Makes a Killer Game?

Some developers are calling it the WOW factor, after the hugely successful *World of Warcraft* enterprise. What makes some games mediocre and forgotten, when others top the charts year after year? There are many special ingredients that go into making your game rise above the rest. We'll now look at some of the most important details of game creation and how you can make your game absolutely killer.

Interactivity

Have you ever played a game that appeared to be one long cut-scene after another, with only short pauses in between where you got to run around as your character before hitting another cut-scene? These games are closer to film projects than really fun games. The reason for this shortcoming is because games are meant to be interactive!

When a player picks up the controller or takes over the keyboard and mouse, she wants to be able to explore make-believe worlds, encounter responsive creatures, and interact with her game environment. If you fail to empower the player with any one of these, you have failed as a game designer.

Interactive Control

Choices that you give players should always be reasonable. Players should never know what's coming; therefore, their choices must not interfere with the game's story. The reason for this is that players are people, and when people are given too much control, they quite predictably act to reduce tension and conflict. And since narrative is dependent on tension and conflict, they can kill the game story before it even gets off the ground.

Tip

"Most narrative forms are vehicles of expression for authors. Games, at their best, are different, allowing a level of collaboration between creator and consumer that's completely unprecedented. Everything in a game story is driven by player choice, by player action."

—Warren Spector, Studio Director, Ion Storm

Reactive Environment

The game world must react reasonably to the game's player. The following are just some of the ways in which game environments respond to players in your everyday game (the majority of games you'll create will fall in the middle two):

- **Adjust the Static**—Books are very static because each time a reader picks one up and reads it the story stays the same. Self-adjusting stories, also called interactive fiction, have branching plotlines based on the reader's choices, like the popular Fighting Fantasy or Choose-Your-Own-Adventure game books.

- **Go Along for the Ride**—Players experience the same events in order every single time they play the game, much like riding a rollercoaster at a theme park.

- **Bumper Cars**—The game world is like one big stage setup, and the players will experience events in new and different ways every time by the way they bump around in them.

- **Improvisation**—Hosting murder mysteries, dinner parties, and role-playing games, like Dungeons and Dragons, all require audience participation and coordination, but they are the hardest to replicate in video games.

Immersion

Have you ever been playing a game when your sibling or parent came up and broke your concentration, and you realized with shock you had been playing it for two hours straight (or more)? Have you ever been playing a game so intently you didn't want to stop? This is because of the key element every game designer wants to foster: immersion. Immersion can cause addictive game play. With immersion, you get so engrossed in a game that for a while you forget it's not real.

The following are the different layers of depth of immersion the gamer feels:

- **Curiosity**—The player feels a slight but fleeting interest in the game.

- **Sympathy**—The player is paying attention to the game but is not personally moved.

- **Identification**—The player identifies with her character and has an invested interest in the outcome.

- **Empathy**—Even though the characters are make-believe, the player shares a strong emotional connection with them.

- **Transportation**—This is the "plenary state" or dream-like trance that you enter into whenever you are really playing a game intensely. The game becomes more real to you than the room you're playing it in.

You will learn that making players care is not always easy. Fashion design guru Marc Ecko broke into the game industry with *Getting Up: Contents Under Pressure* and has a brilliant and methodical mind when it comes to game creation. He calls games "emotional entertainment products" because they are a form of special entertainment—the only form of entertainment that forces players to interact on an emotional level.

Tip

"When emotion is added to a game, then the game will appeal to wider demographics. The game gets better press, gets better buzz, and is more likely to generate allegiance to the brand. The development team will have increased passion for the project. All this translates to increased profits and a much richer game experience."

—David Freeman, *Creating Emotions in Games*

Figure 1.5
David Freeman of the Freeman Group, encouraging *emotioneering* (image courtesy of David Freeman, 2007).

David Freeman (see Figure 1.5) started the Freeman Group, which looks at the many ways you can put emotions into games. Freeman pioneered *emotioneering*, a cluster of techniques seeking to evoke in gamers a breadth and depth of rich emotions. These emotions not only suck the player into the game's world, furthering immersion, but they also form steering points for the designer to guide the player through the game world.

To create emotionally complex moments in your game, consider the following:

- Force the player to do something evil or violate her character's integrity.

- Foster a mysterious or interesting world that takes a while to sort out.

- Give the player ambivalent feelings toward an ally or enemy character, like loving and hating him at the same time.

- Have the other characters recognize or refer to one another as if they were real people.

- Have the player discover she's been tricked or betrayed by an ally.

- Keep the plot twists coming. Remember: "Out of the frying pan, into the fire." Never have a dull moment.

- Set the player up so that she's helpless to aid her friends.

- Set up incongruous events (such as when the main character of *Chrono Cross* suddenly switches places with the main villain and has to gain new allies after losing all his friends).

- Sometimes provide interesting and unexpected consequences to the player's choices.

Challenges

A real game wouldn't be a game if it didn't offer the player a challenge as well as a reactive environment, immersive world, and interactive control. The types of challenges games offer vary widely, from the accumulation of resources to intellectual challenges to survival.

The Game Loop

The most common way players handle difficult challenges is what Andrew Glassner calls the Game Loop (a cycle or repetitive steps the player takes to win a game challenge):

1. Player observes the situation.

2. Player sets goals to win the challenge.

3. Player researches or prepares.

4. Player commits to a plan and executes decisions.

5. Player stops and compares the results of his actions to his original intention.

6. Player evaluates the results.

7. Player returns to step 1.

If you've ever taken a science class, the Game Loop may sound kind of familiar. This is because the Game Loop, which gamers have adopted over years of playing video games, is identical to the scientific method. Scientists use the scientific method to analyze hypotheses. Players use the Game Loop to win games. Seasoned players know that they are not playing the game, but that they have to play against the game's underlying programming. Most of the cheats you find on the Web have been discovered by sharp analytical gamers who figure out what the developers missed.

Competition

Some games may be competitive as well as challenging. There are several different types of competition in games, from playing solo (or solitaire) to playing coop (or in cooperative teams) to playing against one another in a free-for-all. There are also some games, such as Chess, which are zero-sum games; *zero-sum* means that there can be only one winner. If you are playing *Age of Empires* and your goal is to acquire the most resources in your campaign, only one player can acquire the most resources. This makes the game a zero-sum game.

Chance

Chance is that slim margin of luck that can make the gamer a winner or loser. However, chance is not a vague whimsy. The following are types of chances you find in games:

- **Calculated Risk**—The player knows there's a 50/50 chance and takes it.

- **Built-In Chance**—The game's developer sets up parameters for the computer to calculate random odds of the player winning.

- **Player Error**—The player or one of his allies makes a mistake and pays for it.

- **Opponent Error**—The opponent makes a mistake and the player makes sure he pays for it.

- **System Error**—The player discovers a brief flaw in the system and monopolizes on it, winning by cheating. Or the player is betrayed by a computer error setting him back in the game.

No matter the type of chance, luck plays a significant role in the outcome of a game's challenges.

The Four Fs of Great Game Design

There are Four Fs of Great Game Design that are listed in priority and should be considered whenever you have to make any design decision, because they ensure that the game you build will be fantastic. The Four Fs of Great Game Design are Fun, Fairness, Feedback, and Feasibility.

Figure 1.6
For some, letting off a little steam can be fun (image courtesy of Atari, 2007).

Fun

Games can seem like hard work and can sometimes be frustrating to play, but players are willing to put in as much work as required if they get back enough high-quality fun. Fun is what games are all about (see Figure 1.6).

Tip

"I still think that people who make their own games still forget that it's supposed to be fun. I still play enough games where I'm really into it and there's something just amazingly frustrating. Never give your player a reason to put your game down."

—Todd Howard, Bethesda Softworks

If you find that your game is not providing the player with high-quality fun, you have to stop, rewind, and erase what you're doing right now and start building your game on the premise that every part of it has to be fun. A typical rule of thumb when making games is, if you are not having fun making the game, your players probably won't have fun playing it. Enjoy what you do. Come up with crazy off-the-wall ideas that leave you wanting to play your game the second you get it made, and you will have a great game.

Fairness

A player's time must be respected. A great game should offer the quickest easiest ways to have fun and accomplish all the challenges—unless there is some really entertaining reason to prevent it. Make all the player's choices clear. If the player is asked to make a decision, she must be given enough information to make an informed one.

Endless repetition can be absolutely maddening, so don't let your player fall into a rut. Never set the player up so that he has to perform a complicated set of maneuvers to get his little avatar to the top of a 100-foot platform, only at the last minute having it fall all the way back down to the bottom and making him start all over again. A player's experiences through the game should always feel new, yet the player should never know ahead of time what is coming.

Avoid frustration by making the game easier for the player. Don't remove challenges from the game completely, but relieve the build-up of tension that could potentially lose the player's attention.

Feedback

Feedback is just one of the primary components of the human-computer interface. Providing the player with adequate feedback will help the player know what to expect out of the game and frames the choices she will make from then on.

Don't hold back too long on the carrots, or your player will eventually give up. If you want the player to defeat all the Orcs in a single level of the game, you have to give that player some reason for doing so; and when she does beat the Orcs (especially depending on how long and hard it takes to do so), you have to give her some really significant reward, like loud fanfare, gold coins, or power-ups. Likewise, if you don't want your player to do something, like hack up innocent bystanders, you have to set up punishments.

Harvey Smith of Ion Storm gave some terrific presentations at the annual Game Developers Conference in 2003 about game terminology. He defines feedback in this way: "Information communicating the state of the game to the player, usually in response to the player's actions. For instance, text appearing on the screen saying, 'You are fatigued,' which is an old-school way to communicate that the player is running short on 'endurance points' or something. Similarly, showing the player-character avatar suddenly breathing in a laborious fashion, bent over using an 'exhausted' animation, would be a more elegant form of the same feedback."

Feasibility

Anything goes as long as it's fun, fair, provides adequate feedback, and it makes sense.

You might say, "Most games don't make a whole lot of sense!" I understand that. Take *Super Mario Bros.*, for example. You play an overweight plumber who runs around killing strolling mushrooms and kamikaze turtles by squishing them with his own body weight. Meanwhile you have to navigate giant pipes and flaming pits in a world full of titanic toadstools and platforms in the clouds, all to face off with a giant redhead turtle to win a princess in pink named Peach. The game doesn't try to make a lot of sense, but it is fun and it is also consistently feasible.

If you set up your game so that yellow coins give the player boosts to her health, then every time the player sees a yellow coin she will try to reach it. If suddenly coins start doing the opposite of what is expected with no good reason (in this scenario, start hurting the player), then the player will grind her teeth in frustration. Keep your game rules consistently feasible.

Great Game Genres

Now that you have learned the Four Fs of Great Game Design, let's look at what games are "inside the box"—the game types that have become traditional genres—and what they are made of.

Tip

> "I tend to de-emphasize genre in my designing and thinking. I feel that genre is a bit of a double-edged sword for designers. On one hand, genres give designers and publishers a common language for describing styles of play . . . . On the other hand, genres tend to restrict the creative process and lead designers toward tried-and-true gameplay solutions. I encourage students to consider genre when thinking about their games from a business perspective, but not to allow it to stifle their imagination during the design process."
>
> —Tracy Fullerton, Assistant Professor, Electronic Arts Interactive Entertainment Program at USC School of Cinema-Television

Action Games

Action games are made up of all the kinds of games where the player's reflexes and hand-eye coordination make a difference in whether she wins or loses. The most popular action games include the following:

- **First-Person Shooters**—Seen through the eyes of the main character, these games focus on fast-paced movement through detailed game levels, shooting and blowing up everything in sight.

- **Third-Person Shooters**—The player sees the action through a camera, which is aimed from behind the main character or over its shoulder. These games still focus on shooting and blowing stuff up, but the character is always visible onscreen and may have additional controls, like jumping, climbing, and performing martial arts.

- **Platform Jumpers**—The player's character is seen onscreen, sometimes from a side angle. The action no longer focuses on shooting and blowing up bad guys; instead, the main action focuses on the character running and jumping from one platform to the next in a fast-paced animated world.

- **Racing Games**—Racing games feature fast vehicles along nasty tracks and difficult terrain in an all-out race to the finish line.

- **Sports Games**—Featuring rules and scenarios just like the real-world counterpart games, sports games focus on (what did you expect?) sports. Popular sports found in video games include golf, soccer, basketball, football, volleyball, and baseball, but any pastime can be a prospective electronic game.

- **Fighting Games**—Fighting games have the player competing against a single opponent in an arena, where they must duke it out using feet and fists in elaborate combination moves (see Figure 1.7).

- **Stealth Games**—For those players who don't like to rush into battle, there are games that reward the players for sneaking into and out of places without being seen and striking silently.

Adventure Games

One of the first original computer games ever made, with a history as far back as *Zork* and *King's Quest,* adventure games primarily focus on story, exploration, and mental challenges. Most, if not all, adventure games don't even have violent combat in them. Many are mystery games, forcing players to put clues together, like jigsaw pieces, to unravel secrets (see Figure 1.8).

Role-Playing Games

Role-playing games, or RPGs, got their start in pencil and paper in the 1970s with Gary Gygax's Dungeons and Dragons. Since the first teens started with "I want to

Figure 1.7
A street brawler with a hip-hop license (*Def Jam: Icon*, image courtesy of EA Games, 2007).

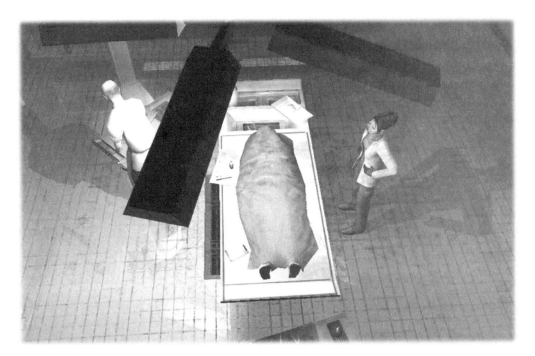

Figure 1.8
Forensic mystery taken to a whole new level (*Fahrenheit: Indigo Prophecy*, image courtesy of Atari, 2005).

Figure 1.9
The popular RPG *World of Warcraft* (image courtesy of Blizzard Entertainment, 2004).

be a wizard!" to today's more complex computer role-playing games, like *Neverwinter Nights, Asheron's Call, World of Warcraft,* and *EverQuest,* players have enjoyed the pretend worlds RPGs offer because of the level of immersion capable in them (see Figure 1.9). Players create their own characters from scratch, and the goal of the game is often making their characters stronger and finding better weapons.

One of the main resources you see in almost every RPG is Experience. Players get Experience for completing missions and beating monsters, and they spend Experience to raise their character's skills or gain new powers. Another popular part of RPGs is communicating with non-player characters, or NPCs, through multiple-choice conversations called *dialogue trees.* Depending on what players decide to say to NPCs, they might make friends or they might find the NPCs rushing them with swords drawn.

Strategy Games

Strategy games envelop a great deal of mental challenge–based games, including real-time strategy (RTS) games, turn-based strategy (TBS) games, and construction-management simulations (CMS). In each, the core play has the player building an empire, fortress, realm, world, or other construct, managing the resources therein, and preparing against inevitable problems like decay, hardship, economic depravity, revolution, or foreign invaders.

Other Game Genres

Besides the game genres already mentioned, there are many more:

- **Casual Games**—Chess, Poker, Texas Hold 'em, Solitaire, mah-jongg, trivia games, and others share a clustered category under casual or traditional games.

- **Online Games**—Any game played through an Internet connection, including Xbox Live Arcade games, are considered online games. Ones with lots of players joining together in coop or versus modes in the same game realms are called massive multiplayer online games, or MMOs.

- **Artificial Life Games**—The player of an A-life game cares for a creature or virtual pet. Neopets is best known for the minding of your very own Neopet. In Nintendogs, players can feed, play, and care for virtual canines.

- **Puzzle Games**—These games never have much of a story. Instead, they focus on mental challenges alone. Examples include Bejeweled and Tetris.

- **Advertainment Games**—These are games whose primary purpose it is to advertise a brand or service. Lots of companies are now putting their advertainment games on their Web sites.

- **Serious Games**—Serious games are a serious business; many of them are educational games, which help schools teach subjects in the guise of having fun, or they can be training games, helping companies to instruct their employees in specific tasks.

Tip

"One of the more interesting trends today is the plethora of 'mixed-genre' games. It seems that one way to mitigate risk, while still trying to innovate, is to take several popular genres . . . and mix them to create a new style of game. *Deus Ex* is a great example of this hybrid."

—Tracy Fullerton, Assistant Professor, Electronic Arts
Interactive Entertainment Program at USC School of Cinema-Television

Ways to Come Up with Killer Game Ideas

You probably already have a great idea for a game that you can't wait to make. If you don't or are uncertain how to come up with an idea, here are some tricks to brainstorm ideas:

- Take a retro classic 2D sprite game, like the ones on the early Nintendo or SEGA consoles, and make it a vast searchable 3D game (or vice versa—take a huge 3D game and try converting it to a much simpler 2D sprite game).

- Choose one of your all-time-favorite games from the past and clone it using new technology.

- Pick a game that you really like and tear it apart. Don't do it literally, of course. Choose what you like about it, what you don't like about it, and what could have been done to make the game better.

- Watch a movie or read a book. Think about the possibilities. Could it be adapted into a game? What genre would it be? How would it play?

- Ask your friends what kinds of games they would want to play.

- Play lots of different games. If you usually play sports games, try a role-playing game. Feel the field.

Remember that most of the ideas out there have been done over and over, and that there are no entirely new ideas. It doesn't matter. You need to put your spin on the world. Take an existing idea and make it better. That is your goal as a game designer.

Review

At the end of reading this chapter, you should know:

- What a game designer does.

- What a game designer goes through to create a game.

- Who indie game developers are and how you can become one.

- That a great game must be immersive, reactive, and challenging.

- How to make a winning game based on the Four Fs of Great Game Design.

- What game genres are out there right now.

- How to come up with your own original game ideas.

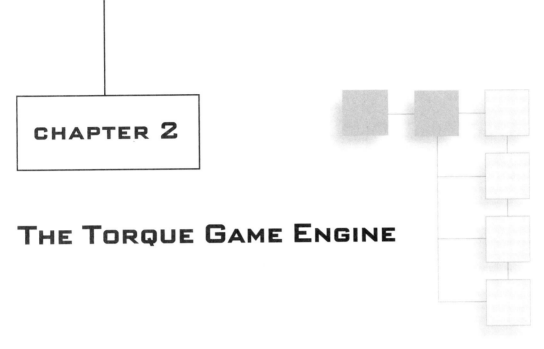

CHAPTER 2

THE TORQUE GAME ENGINE

The founders of GarageGames, including Damon Slye, Jeff Tunnel, Rick Overman, and Tim Gift, previously ran a game development company called Dynamix that got started in 1984 and made games such as *Earthsiege, Starsiege, Tribes,* and *Tribes 2.* The Torque Game Engine, or TGE, is a modified version of a 3D computer game engine originally developed by Dynamix for their 2001 first-person shooter game *Tribes 2* (see Figure 2.1). Their AAA 3D game engine is one of the most comprehensive and affordable on the market today, and a license to use it is available from GarageGames, an Internet game publishing label based in Eugene, Oregon.

GarageGames' name is purposefully based on the term "garage band." Many game companies start as "garage outfits" by a bunch of friends getting together to

Figure 2.1
Tribes 2 was so popular it was purchased by Sierra Studios (image courtesy of Sierra Studios, 2001).

create entertaining indie titles for fun and not so much for profit. The number one goal of GarageGames is to offer licensing of game engines and publishing to these indie developers, which means you!

Games Made with Torque

TGE is consistently ranked number one on the Top 10 Commercial Engines listed on DevMaster.net. Game designers have been proving time and again that the Torque Game Engine works, making the list of games created using TGE an exponentially growing one (see Figure 2.2). At the time of this writing, the list of game titles made with TGE includes the following:

Age of Time

Blockland

Figure 2.2
Just a glance at the games made with Torque.

Buccaneer: The Pursuit of Infamy

Dark Horizons: Lore Invasion

Desert Gunner

Dimenxian

Golden Fairway

Magecraft

Marble Blast Gold

Minigolf Mania

Minions of Mirth

Once Upon A Time

Orbz

PCD Music Lounge

Penny Arcade Adventures: On the Rain-Slick Precipice of Darkness

RocketBowl

Sachi's Quest

Shelled!

Shokrok Throwdown

ThinkTanks

TubeTwist

Ultimate Duck Hunting

Wildlife Tycoon: Venture Africa

Torque's Features at a Glance

Your first impression might be that the Torque Game Engine appears to target the making of shooter action games, but this belies the true power of TGE. Sure, you can make a shooter game, and you will, following the tutorials in this book, but you can also create a game of any genre, in 2D or 3D.

Tip

"GarageGames' Torque Game Engine has streamlined our development processes and enabled our teams in the pursuit of our core goal: creating the innovative gameplay that gamers want. Torque gives our programmers a +6 dagger of coding!"

—Joel DeYoung, Hothead COO

The Torque Game Engine has the following features; if there are any that you are unfamiliar with or don't understand, bear with me, because they'll be explained in more detail later on (this is simply a brief overview).

- Torque provides robust scripting, networking code, in-engine world editing, and GUI creation. The source code can be compiled on Windows, Macintosh, and Linux platforms.

- Torque uses TorqueScript for its coding. If you know Flash ActionScript, Visual Basic, or any other scripting language, you will have no problem coding in TorqueScript to make your game. It is easy to learn and flexible.

- Torque allows you to publish games directly to the PC, Macintosh, or Xbox 360 (with a separate license). Use CodeOnce to play them on your computer or console right away.

- Torque is great right out of the box, with all the code needed to render, play, and capture game elements, from 3D graphics and GUIs to sound and Input/Output (I/O).

- Torque features a terrain engine that automatically creates LODs (levels of detail) of the ground surfaces so that it renders the fewest polygons necessary at any given time. Textures applied to the terrain can be blended together seamlessly.

- Torque supports loading of 3D models in the DTS and DIF file formats. DTS models can be animated using skeletal animation or morph target animation; thus DTS models are typically used for characters and vehicles. DIF models have precalculated lighting, so they are less suitable for animation.

- The game's rendering engine features Gouraud shading, environment mapping, volumetric fog, and many other effects, such as decals. (For example, if a player in a Torque-made game fires a weapon that leaves a bullet hole in the wall, the bullet hole is a decal.)

- Torque has been used to make both non-networked single-player games and networked multiplayer games. The Torque Game Engine today is both single-player and multiplayer ready. It is based on standard client-server architecture and is fully scalable up to 128 players and even beyond.

- Torque is both memory and network bandwidth efficient. Torque uses static data blocks for common data and network compression, plus special transmission-reduction algorithms to keep low bandwidth requirements per connection.

- Torque is not traditionally shader-based, but it is set up to easily apply shaders with the Torque Game Engine Advanced (formerly known as the Torque Shader Engine). Torque has fully capable raster-based graphics.

- Torque is designed around event-driven simulation using separate client and server event loops. An event system also drives the game and GUI logic.

- Torque has starter kits for a first-person shooter and an off-road racing game. A real-time strategy starter kit is also available as a separate purchase. These starter packs can be modified to suit your needs, or you can start from scratch.

- Almost anyone can play the games you build with Torque. Because of Torque's unique compatibility, CodeOnce handles most computer platforms. The system is even set to run on Microsoft Windows 98 machines and machines running old Voodoo 3D cards.

Okay, you should be forewarned. Torque is a software development kit, or SDK, and is therefore somewhat daunting at first impression. It has lines of code after lines of code, lots of source files, libraries, demos, kits, resources, and multiple communities that drive it. It is flat out huge. Yet that's what makes it the powerhouse it is, and when all is said and done you can manage it and put yourself in the Game Master's chair.

Torque also comes with one of the best support communities on the Web any indie developer could hope for. The GarageGames community at www.garagegames.com is absolutely superb and driven to providing you with all the help you need to get started. If you have a wish list or a question, take it there. The forums are really well attended, the staff and individuals are knowledgeable, and the GarageGames site provides excellent resources, including scripts, code snippets, links online, reference material, books to help you out, and so much more.

Spotlight on Reiss Rascals Games

"My name is Randel Reiss and I am one of the partners of Prairie Games, Inc, makers of the first indie MMORPG *Minions of Mirth*—based on GarageGames' Torque Game Engine.

Figure 2.3
Reiss Rascals Games at the 2005 IGC.

A year and a half ago, I took my two sons, Kyle and Connor, ages 13 and 11 years old, respectively, at the time, to the 2005 Indie Games Conference in Eugene, Oregon. The conference was sponsored by GarageGames. The key reason why I took my sons there was because they had started their own garage-based game company, which they still run, called Reiss Rascals Games. They've fluently been using Milkshape 3D to create models, textures, skeletons, animations and even rigging (rigging is pretty advanced, as you may know)—then importing them into Torque for their own games.

At the conference, the youngest attendees to date, they showed their latest work to the well-known video game industry producer, Tony Ramos. Tony has produced games for Electronic Arts, Sony, and Sega. During their demonstration, Mark Frohnmayer, then president of GarageGames, original founder and the original lead engineer for *Tribes* and *Tribes 2*, sat in on the presentation." (See Figure 2.3.)

—Randel Reiss

Licensing

As of the Torque Game Engine version 1.5, the Torque Indie License allows the engine to be used by independent game developers for $150 per programmer, provided that said programmer is not employed by a development company with annual revenues of $250,000 or more. You probably don't make $250,000 a year—do you? No. So you won't have to worry about the cost! This licensing model is intended for low-budget designers, as it saves them time and effort of programming their own game engine without requiring a large amount of money to license. Compare that $150 to the $350,000 you would have to pay for the Unreal Engine 2!

The Torque Indie License also requires that you display the GarageGames logo before your game starts up, though this requirement is omitted if you buy the commercial license (the Torque Commercial License is for sale at $749).

You pay no royalties ever with the Torque royalty-free licenses. You can publish your game anywhere you want, whether it's on the Internet or in stores. It's your game, you make the decisions.

Tip

"The general perception in the industry is that the more you pay, the better the product you get. The extra cost buys you, among other things, higher quality, responsive technical support, proper documentation, and so on . . . . So, if you can live without the mothering support that other middleware providers offer, TGE really does measure up in just about every other area. You get the full source code, a rapid response on bug fixes and issues, and tools and technology that are comparable to other costly middleware packages."

—Justin Lloyd

The Torque Game Builder

The Torque Game Builder, sometimes called TGB, Torque 2D, or T2D, is a separate game engine designed for 2D games based on scripts that make up the Torque Game Engine (see Figure 2.4). The name was changed to the Torque Game Builder when a graphical design interface was added on top of the Torque 2D scripting software.

If you want to make classic retro games in 2D, the Torque Game Builder might be more up your alley than using the Torque Game Engine, which is targeted toward 3D game creation. The Torque Game Builder has been used to develop a number of commercially published games, including the following:

Atomize

Fortune Tiles

Gold Fever

Kachinko

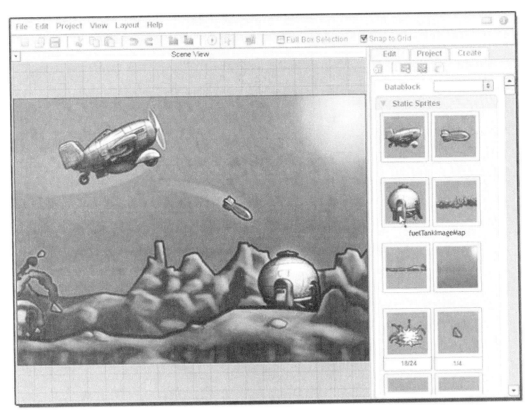

Figure 2.4
The Torque Game Builder.

King Kong: Skull Island Adventure

LEGO: Bricktopia

Phantasia

Puzzle Poker

Rack'em Up Road Trip

Trick Ball

The Torque X Engine

When Microsoft released their award-winning next-generation console system, the Xbox 360, they also opened the doors for indie developers to start creating their own games for use with the console. Now you can create your own games for the Xbox 360 and publish them in the Xbox Live Arcade marketplace.

In order to do this, Microsoft released the XNA Game Studio Express December 11, 2006. The XNA Game Studio Express uses C# program code to design both Xbox 360 console games and Windows PC games. The same day the XNA Game Studio Express came out, GarageGames released a beta of their concept technology, the Torque X.

Torque X actually allows users of the Torque Game Builder to make games portable to the Xbox 360. The Torque X Open Beta is in binary, but it comes with demo versions of the TGB editors tailored for use with Torque X, as well as some example games and starter kits. Torque X Pro will have full source code and more control. So far, only 2D games are capable of being made with it, using the Torque Game Builder system, but 3D support is on the way.

To share your games with the rest of the world for Xbox 360 using Torque X, you must be a member of the XNA Creators Club. The XNA Creators Club is set up by Microsoft for users to port their games to the proprietary console machine. You can find out more about the XNA Creators Club online at http://msdn.microsoft.com/xna/creators.

The Torque Game Engine Advanced

If you were an experienced programmer ready to make truly amazing next-generation games with the hottest game technology available, then you would need the next level of Torque. Torque Game Engine Advanced lets you do dramatic visuals and beautiful high-quality effects, on top of an underlying foundation of physics, networking, scripting, animation, and the rest of the game engine—to get your professional game developed in record time to meet your milestones and at a fraction of the cost.

Torque Game Engine Advanced, or TGEA, rests on the original Torque Game Engine; but TGEA has support for modern shaders and a much more tailored rendering engine to improve the look and efficiency to make it easy for you to create pure eye candy. This engine empowers you to do it all.

The MMO Workshop

Prairie Games, the makers of *Minions of Mirth,* has worked in conjunction with the folks at GarageGames in the development and release of the MMO

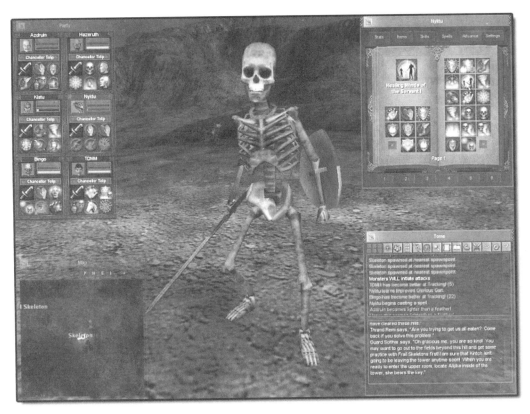

Figure 2.5
You can create online RPGs like *Minions of Mirth* (image courtesy of Prairie Games, 2007).

Workshop, or Torque MMO Kit. The Torque MMO Kit is a commercially proven, completely ready solution for Torque users who want to make massive multiplayer online games similar to *Minions of Mirth* (which, by the way, featured something over 35,000 registered players). See Figure 2.5.

There is tie-in support for the Torque Game Engine Advanced, and developers are not restricted to a multiplayer online game platform at all; in fact, the MMO Kit comes ready to make a single-player game simultaneously with a multiplayer option!

The MMO Kit runs off C++, Python, and TorqueScript. I will discuss these languages in more detail in Chapter 10, "Me Game, You Mission." You can find out more about the MMO Workshop online at www.mmoworkshop.com/trac/mom/wiki/FAQ.

Built-In Components of Torque

All the Torque Game Engines share a unique suite of tools in their tool kits that empower you to build the very best indie games you can. These include TorqueScript, TorqueNet, CodeOnce, GeoTerrain, Torque Lighting System, Doorway, and Puppeteer Mesh Animation.

TorqueScript

TorqueScript is a really easy-to-use scripting language, along the lines of C++. (TorqueScript has similar object-oriented logic, and several programmers prefer to use C++ instead of TorqueScript for their games, which is fine.) TorqueScript brings together all the elements of your game. Most of your game can be programmed in TorqueScript, and additions, such as engine physics or tougher enemy AI coded in C++, can be called from the script. The separate IDE tool, Torsion, allows you to program faster in TorqueScript and in a more focused way. Torsion is provided for you on the companion CD, but Torsion is only for Windows users. You could also choose Codeweaver, which is a free development tool for TorqueScript editing; you can find out more about Codeweaver online at www.torquedev.com/download.php. Personally, I favor the use of Notepad to do basic text editing.

TorqueNet

All Torque games default to a client-server architecture. This delivers more consistent gameplay by reducing a player's ability to "hack in" and gain advantages within your project. Since you act as the server, you are the main authoritative data owner because only the server administrator can make direct changes to simulated objects in the game. Players are given only the information needed to observe the game environment through their player character's point of view.

CodeOnce

Write your game on any platform, and then port it to Windows, Mac OS X, or Linux within hours. Under Torque X, you must have an XNA Creators Club membership before porting your game to the Xbox 360.

GeoTerrain

GeoTerrain is a built-in terrain generator in the Mission Builder of Torque. It allows for the creation of seamless blended terrain with texture maps and light

Figure 2.6
Showing off some event-driven lighting (*Dark Horizons: Lore Invasion,* image courtesy of Max Gaming Technologies, LLC, 2007).

maps and altitude-based fog banks. It allows you, the creator, to manipulate every aspect of the terrain for more realism.

Torque Lighting System

Enhanced lighting and rendering algorithms create brighter and more vibrant worlds. You can get some really neat special effects, such as overexposure and specular highlighting. You can also use harder contrast in levels to get sharper light and shadows. Simultaneous rendering of lights on static objects to create dynamic shadows and mission lights to change the lighting in an environment based upon events (see Figure 2.6) provide you with some amazingly realistic variations.

Doorway

Interior environments define large objects, such as buildings and open spaces that players and entities can move around in. These environments are stored in a native format called DIF, which uses a Binary Space Partition (BSP) collision scheme similar to that found in any Quake-based game engine. Torque seamlessly integrates these environments with the terrain engine. You can whip together DIFs using the Torque Constructor, QuArK, or any other Valve 220 MAP editing program. We'll take a further look at DIFs in Chapter 6, "Interior Design Isn't for Decorators."

Puppeteer Mesh Animation

You may not know much about 3D rigging and animation just yet, but let me tell you that the Puppeteer system Torque offers is one of the smoothest in terms of skeletal animation. It allows for assigning vertices (or intersection points) of the model's wire mesh to joints of bones and assigns weights to each, which in layman's speech means you get better character models because they bend more realistically.

The Torque 3D Toolset

What you will use most when tinkering in Torque are the editors. Each editor is a WYSIWYG (what-you-see-is-what-you-get) tool that lets you get dirty messing with the individual parts of your game levels. You can edit every aspect of your world, including weather, fog, terrain attributes, simulated objects, and events, all in the World Editor. You can make your own interfaces, write custom player controls, and edit and test your game all without leaving the GUI Editor. And there is so much more. Following are some descriptions of the tools you will be using.

World Editor

The World Editor is an in-game tool that includes eight sub-editors, each integrated to provide the foundations for creating, modifying, and saving the various parts of your game. The major components of the World Editor are the World Editor sub-editors and the Terrain Editor sub-editors. We'll cover the World Editor in Chapter 5, "Wide Open Spaces."

World Editor Sub-Editors

The World Editor sub-editors offer you a powerful object placement kit for building game scenes and structures. You can create, place, size, scale, and rotate individual objects, as well as view and modify any of the properties of those objects. Select an object, and you can easily edit all its parameters via text boxes, spinners, radio buttons, and checkboxes.

Terrain Editor Sub-Editors

Terrain is the basis for the large outdoor areas seen in Torque games. Torque represents open landscapes using a height-map to determine elevation, and it can blend up to six textures together over the terrain's surface. The Terrain Editor consists of the Terrain Terraformer, Terrain Texture Editor, and Terrain Texture Painter. The Terrain Editor is an awesome sculpting tool that gives you unprecedented direct control over the shape the ground terrain will take. The terrain editor also lets you manually adjust textures, place them, and blend them, or choose from a whole palette of textures and paint directly onto the terrain, as if it were a canvas.

GUI Editor

If you didn't already know, GUI stands for Graphical User Interface. The interface is how the player of a game interacts with the machine that is running the game (including all Input/Output, or I/O). It handles all controls (windows, buttons, text fields, menus, HUDs, and more) that make up this interface.

The GUI Editor is righteous to use, including a simple drag-and-drop creator. Torque's GUI system lets you create most any interface you can imagine. Designing intuitive, easily navigable interfaces that gamers interact with is a huge part of game design, and knowing how to use the GUI Editor to its fullest becomes a primary focus in your path to building a successful game of your own. We'll look at using the GUI Editor in Chapter 8, "Getting Gooey (GUI)."

Resources

The CD-ROM that comes with this book will provide you with the trial version of the Torque Game Engine SDK version 1.5; but if you are really sold on the software, you should go online and get your own copy of this state-of-the-art game engine. Although the majority of this text will focus on game creation using the Torque Game Engine, many of the same principles apply to making games in general, with any game engine.

The CD-ROM also has programs that we'll be using to create our graphic assets and sound files. These programs are not shipped with or related to Torque in any fashion, but they are necessary for the production pipeline. They include Paint Dot Net, Audacity, and Blender.

Figure 2.7
Marino Sounds share with you sound experiences for your game creation.

In this book, you will create your very own 3D game, called *Abandon All Hope*, using Torque. To assist you, there are project files on the CD for the chapters where you find the projects. Some of these resource files are special licensed demos from other companies not associated with Torque:

- **Tridinaut**—This free model pack is an exclusive sampling of 3D models in the native DTS format. Find out more about Tridinaut online at www.tridinaut.com.

- **Frogames**—There are four different model packs, including samples from the Dungeon Guardians, Dungeon, RTS Buildings for Humans, and RTS Buildings for Orcs. Each has DTS models, texture files, sprite files, DIF objects, and more. Find out more about Frogames online at www.frogames.net.

- **Marino Sounds**—For your listening delight, there are music compositions and sound effects (featuring gun sounds and bursts, as well as medieval weaponry). Find out more about Marino Sounds at www.manuelmarino.com (see Figure 2.7).

Review

After reading this chapter you should know

- How the Torque Game Engine (TGE) got started.

- What the basic features of Torque are.

- How to license Torque to make your own games.

- What the optional editions of Torque are called and what they do.

- What the major components of Torque are, including TorqueScript, TorqueNet, and more.

- How the 3D toolset is set up to aid you in creating games in a WYSIWYG interface.

- What resources this book comes with to help you use Torque to make your own games.

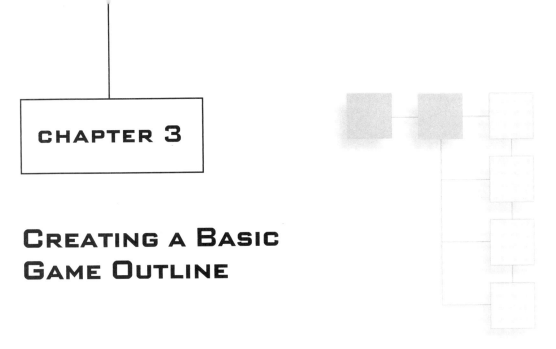

CHAPTER 3

CREATING A BASIC GAME OUTLINE

As mentioned in Chapter 1 ("So You Want to Be a Game Designer?"), game developers never work in a void. They always have a road map, obviously depicting where they are headed. This typically falls under the control of a project manager or lead game designer on a team.

In most cases, it's considered good practice to write down your game outline before you ever start to build. Most production will be fluid, meaning that changes can occur at any time, but it never hurts to know where you are going so you don't get lost along the way.

First you will see what it takes to make a game outline, and then you will be given an example game outline.

Game Design Document

Each game design document, or GDD, is set up and handled differently for each individual game project. However, there are some basics. Typically a GDD does two things:

- **Reveals Details**—If it isn't specified in the GDD, it isn't getting done. The GDD tells the development team every tedious detail that will go into the game, like "Put feature B at position X and Y, and hook it up to widget C."

■ **Conveys Vision**—The GDD can sometimes sound like a proposal. It has a load of "Let me tell you a tale about widget C and why it's so cool."

Some writers of GDDs can get a little too exhaustive on the details, creating dreary monstrosities that are ponderous to carry around and even worse to have to read. Today's developers are starting to use electronic tools to make GDDs, including online blogs or wiki (which enables them to have interlinked pages; so if a designer wants more information about a feature, he can click and jump to another page to read more about it).

No matter the medium you decide to write your GDD in, the following are typical sections you should carry over.

Game Overview

After coming up with a killer game idea, you will need to set out your objectives for your game project. Many developers do this through the creation of a game overview. The game overview is often the cornerstone of a game project's build, and without it the project has a shaky foundation.

Creating Your Objectives

Draft objectives based on what you want to see come of your game idea. When writing your objectives, you should follow the SMART methodology as defined by James Lewis in his book, *Fundamentals of Project Management* (American Management Association, 2002).

Make each objective

■ Specific

■ Measurable

■ Attainable

■ Realistic

■ Time-Limited

Target Audience

Next, define your target audience. You cannot create something unless you know who you are creating it for. In other words, who are the players of your proposed game supposed to be? In many cases, it is all right to make a game for yourself. If you have fun playing the game, then chances are good there are niche markets of people out there just like you who will love the game, too. However, to truly reach a broad market, you will be better off considering the following:

- **Geographics**—Where your target audience lives. Where do you think they live? Are they in the United States, United Kingdom, or elsewhere? Are they in big cities or small rural towns?

- **Demographics**—Statistics about your audience, like age, gender, and income. Where do you think those in your audience fit? Are they young or old? Male or female? Do they come from an upper-income, middle-income, or lower-income family?

- **Psychographics**—Values, attitudes, and beliefs of your audience. What kind of ethics do they adhere to, do you think? Is killing wrong, or is it right? What does your audience believe?

Scope of the Project

No, I am not talking about mouthwash. To determine the scope of your game, you must look at the big picture. You should determine the following:

- **Platform**—Is the game going to be developed primarily for the computer or console platform?

- **Genre**—What is the game's primary genre (for example, is it a first-person shooter, RPG, strategy game, or something else)?

- **Player Mode**—Is the game primarily a single-player or multiplayer game?

- **Player POV**—Which camera perspective will be forced through most of the game (for example, first-person, third-person, or other)?

- **Content**—What content should be included in your game?

- **Style**—What is the overall aesthetic style of the game? What will its look and color scheme be like? What kind of mood do you want to affect?

- **Interface**—How will users navigate through the information? What types of interfaces will be required? How will the interface components be laid out?

- **Time Interval**—Will the game be real-time, turn-based, or time-limited?

- **Audio**—How will audio be used in the game (for instance, music, sound effects, dialogue, and compositions)?

- **Technology**—What technology will be required to create the game? If you are using Torque, what limitations with the software will you have to overcome?

Tip

Each game project is unique. Remember that your game can only be as successful as the preparation put into it. Determine the scope of your game before moving on, and never make assumptions about the project. If you leave any gray areas, you might get lost in them later on—so be careful.

Answer FAQs

Everyone has questions about the game, including the folks who may give you the funds to make it and the teams of designers who may offer to help you build it. What was not answered clearly in the game overview should be stabbed at here.

What Is the Game?

Describe the game in a single simple paragraph. This is the answer to the most common question that you will be asked, including by your mom. What are you working on?

Why Create This Game?

Why are you creating this game? Do you love military-based shooters? Do you think there is a gap in the market for another zombie game? Do more RPGs need to have magic-casting elves in them?

Where Does the Game Take Place?

Describe the world that your game takes place in. It's as simple as that. Help frame it in the reader's mind by spending a paragraph on it here. Later, you can go into it in more lengthy detail in a section dedicated to describing the world.

What Do I Control?

Describe what (or who) the player will control in the course of the game.

What Is the Point?

Now that you know where the game is going to take place and what (or who) the player controls, the next big question is what are they supposed to achieve in this world? Are they doing something as clichéd as "saving the world"? Are they trying to amass the largest ore mines? What?

What's So Different about This Game?

This question comes up a lot. Tell them what is different from the hundreds of competitive games attempting to break into this market right now. If you can't think of anything, be honest. Say "This is just another Pac-Man clone, but it was done by me, so it's cool!"

Spotlight on Mode 7 Games

Mode 7 Games is the small indie game company responsible for *Determinance,* the sword-fighting third-person game made with the Torque Game Engine (see Figure 3.1). As they say, "We believe in creating fun, intelligently tactical action games and releasing them at a minimal cost to gamers. If you're interested in our work in any way, we'd love to talk to you." Mode 7 Games' core team is made up of two people: Ian Hardingham and Paul Taylor.

After graduating in 2003, Ian Hardingham started Mode 7 Games to explore his interest in creating a multiplayer game. Ian is the lead designer, producer, and programmer on *Determinance.* Paul Taylor began his association with Mode 7 by working on *Determinance*'s music and sound but is now responsible for PR and future efforts at Mode 7.

Determinance *is a pretty unique game. What is so unusual about it, first of all, is the sword fighting. How did Mode 7 Games come up with that idea, and how easy was it to implement in* Torque*?*

IAN: "I've always wanted to make a sword-fighting game where the mouse controls the sword: I wanted it to be all about the geometry and not just about triggering combos. The thing about an

Figure 3.1
Determinance by Mode 7 Games (image courtesy of Mode 7 Games, 2007).

engine that's as fully featured as Torque is that, on the plus side, you get a load of features you really need; however, when implementing new features, you have to do the added work of understanding everything about the engine first and making sure the features are implemented in a 'Torque-consistent' manner. One of the reasons we chose Torque is because we wanted a mid-number-of-players multiplayer game that had flying in it, good collision, and large outdoor environments. Torque is perfect for this. The majority of the work was on the player skeleton and muscle systems, which were in fact very easy to integrate into Torque's player system."

How difficult or easy were the Torque editors to use, and did you use TorqueScript, C++, Python, or another programming language to script Determinance?

IAN: "The Torque level editor is very easy to use and, while it lacks some features of other editors, it really did the job for us. The Torque GUI Editor and the GUI system in general are truly superb and industry-leading. We used TorqueScript, although I was tempted by Python. I like Torque-Script—it allows you to write game mechanics very easily. *Determinance* had an unusually high amount of low-level engine coding in C++, and we ran into Torque's general bloatedness a few times; however, the advantages of all the small, but completely necessary, features that Torque includes outweigh this particular disadvantage. *Determinance* is an online game, and our backend services are written in Python using Twisted and SQL Alchemy."

A lot of indie developers work on a small scale and team members have to multitask to get the job done. Were there any conflicts of team work? Did you have a team leader or project manager to maintain creative vision?

PAUL: "Ian took charge of project management as well as design and development for the vast majority of the time it took us to develop the game. I originally joined the team to do the music, but I later ended up taking over some parts of the business, such as PR and marketing, as well as assisting Ian with getting resources and so on. Ian would actually have melted from stress and then resolidified into some kind of odd human cheese if I hadn't done this. By the end, once we had the assets in place, it was mostly just us and our testers working on getting the game into shape, and having a more pared-down team towards the end certainly helped."

IAN: "Absolutely. The real challenge was to get people who weren't being paid to do work when they didn't feel like it. I had to approach each individual differently to achieve this, and most of them are still talking to me."

What advice would you give to teens looking to become indie developers themselves?

PAUL: "Ian's better qualified to talk about design and programming, but if you want to be an artist or a musician working on games, all I can say is get good at what you do and get noticed for doing it. Look at professional-quality art in your chosen medium and work out how it was done, find out how you can do something of that standard, and then learn to do it better. Set small goals and be ruthlessly persistent in achieving them. When you feel you're at a high standard, look at ways of getting into the industry. Most people will be happiest working in a mainstream games company at first to learn their craft. If that's not for you, then try to find other like-minded people! If you're an amazing artist, we might need you, so drop us a line via our Web site and show us your portfolio."

IAN: "Artists, modelers, and musicians: find an indie team, and do what they ask of you to a professional standard. Coders: make a small, not-too-ambitious mod in Torque to get a general feel for what's going on, and then start assembling a team. If you want to design a game, you'd better learn coding, because until you can pay one, you won't find a coder who will do what you want."

What advice would you give to someone just starting to use Torque?

PAUL: "Get help from other Torque users at GarageGames and elsewhere. It's invaluable."

IAN: "Start off by taking five of the most popular code resources on GarageGames and implement them carefully, doing your level best to understand what's going on at all stages. Start implementing something not too ambitious. Whenever you come across a Torque system, don't be impatient; take a couple of hours to research and try and understand it. Those couple of hours will save you days. As for what Paul said, try to ask questions intelligently, and make sure you're doing as much work as you are asking someone to do by helping you. People will not do anything for you, but if you ask nicely, they will help you out."

You can read more about Mode 7 games online at www.mode7games.com.

Feature Set

This section of your GDD should document exactly what special features you have decided to put into your game. List all the essential selling points about your game right here. If they are purely technical features, then you can leave them for the technical specs section later on.

The feature set should also depict how the player plays the game and what the highlights of the gameplay experience will be. Think about it for a moment. If you have nothing to put here, is this game really worth doing?

Work Breakdown

A work breakdown simply breaks down your game project into tasks and sub-tasks, assigns team members to those tasks, and estimates hours it will take to get those tasks done.

Task Determination

Tasks can be either specific or general to the project.

- Specific tasks are steps needed to complete a feature of the finished project. A feature may be a player character. To create this character, you or your team need to write a character description, draw concept artwork, create a 3D model, and animate the character in motion. Each of these is a specific task.

- General tasks include the broad steps applied to almost every feature within your product to create the best player interface, style, story, and gameplay—including quality assurance.

Estimating a Timeline

Once you have generated all your tasks, you begin estimating the duration it will take to complete each one.

There are interdependencies that can stand in the way of progress. You cannot begin play-testing until all the assets are in place, and you cannot finish the assets until the concept artwork has been reviewed. You cannot finalize the enemy AI until the first prototype is finished. Steps like these are points in a project in which nothing else can be accomplished until that step has been completed. These points are considered milestones, but they can also become bottlenecks if you don't figure them into your timeline properly.

One of the ways that game companies discover a timeline is by developing a working game prototype. A prototype that isn't all that great to look at but has most of the conceptual ideas worked out into feasible features can set an estimated deadline for when the fully realized game will be done. Many game companies start with a prototype and build around it.

Estimating Costs

Your next step is to identify costs. Game development requires the integration of art, design, writing, audio, and programming elements into a seamless package. In a "garage" game outfit, people share multiple design roles in this production.

Of course, your cost can be as low as nothing if you have a place, a computer, the right software, and the time to do all the work yourself. Otherwise, cost factors can include

- **Employees**—Costs associated with your team, including salary, benefits, bonuses, and reimbursements.

- **Talents and Licensing**—Outsourced staff or companies (such as composers, writers, VFX artists, or voiceover talents).

- **Equipment**—Servers, workstations, networking equipment, scanner beds, digital cameras, printers, and software packages that you need to complete the game project.

- **Overhead**—Cost of maintaining your office and work environment, such as rent, utilities, and office supplies.

Asset Production

Most asset production is done through a collaboration of designers, going from sketches to wiremesh to 3D models and virtual terrain. Typically you should have some of the major assets halfway completed before starting to script a game so that programmers will have something to test with.

The Game World

This is the area where you provide an overview of the game world. Break down the game world into smaller component pieces, often game levels, and describe what's so important about each of them. Most game level designers will offer top-down maps of each of the environments, and writers will offer physical descriptions and key locations.

Some things to remember when designing a game world are

- **Climate**—Is it day or night? Is it wet and rainy, snowing, or fair?

- **Lighting**—How is the area going to be lit, and what are the light sources?

- **Objects**—Here you must spell out the main objects, power-ups, and items found in each location.

- **Scale**—Describe how big each area is supposed to be.

- **Theme**—Indicate if there should be a specific style, mood, or gimmick to the location.

- **Travel**—How does the player move characters around the game map?

The Game Characters

Describe not only the player's character(s) but also ally characters, enemy characters, monsters, bosses, and more. Provide statistics and descriptions of each. The more onscreen time a character gets, the more details you should furnish. If the player can change or customize her character, you had better describe how that works in this section.

The Game Items

Write a brief overview of each of the items players might find and use in the game, including weapons, inventory items, puzzle pieces, keys, ammo, or power-ups. Items should be depicted by concept artwork and given unique looks based on the game's style before they are created in 3D.

Interface Design

A game interface designer must understand how to display information visually so that players understand how to play the game. A designer typically uses a navigational flowchart to document the interface and how the player would navigate the game. Most interface designers use simple flowcharting software packages, such as Microsoft Word or Visio, to get started. We will look at interface design further in Chapter 8, "Getting Gooey (GUI)."

Sound Design

Take a shot at describing in words what sound will be included in the game. Some composed music can be triggered by events or set to specific game environments. You should also consider the sounds used for special effects, including weapons fire and dialogue voiceovers. The sound engineering in a game is very particular, and we will cover it in more detail in Chapter 9, "The Sound and The Fury" (see Figure 3.2).

Technical Specs

The technical specs include information like target platform or screen resolution, and it also outlines peripheral requirements. Make sure your GDD includes the following:

- **Database, Server, or Network**—Will a database be needed? What platform or version is preferable?

- **Development Software**—What software will be needed by the programming team, art team, and design team?

- **Display**—Screen resolution, bit number of colors, or monitor size.

- **Internet**—If the game will target the online platform, what is the expected access speed, browser type, and other ISP-related needs?

- **Platform**—Will the target platform for the game be computer, console, online, or arcade? If the game targets a computer platform, what are the minimum and recommended requirements (involving operating system, processor speed, memory, or hard disk space)?

- **Security**—What level of security is needed?

Figure 3.2
The audio mixing and sound lab at High Moon Studios (image courtesy of High Moon Studios, 2007).

Example

Figures 3.3 through 3.5 are excerpts from the initial game proposal for the popular adventure game *Myst*, as designed by Rand and Robyn Miller, which was finally accepted by Broderbund. Game proposals derive most of their content from the GDD but are mostly sales pitches to get a game accepted by a publisher, production company, or investor. Take a look at what went into the making of *Myst*.

Example   55

MYST
Game Design Proposal

General description:

Myst, in essence, is a mystery. There are two main characters in the Myst world. It is the player's objective to deduce which of these two characters is guilty of a crime and which is innocent. The player acts as both detective and judge. Using the clues found in the Myst world, the player uses his or her own logic and intelligence to navigate throughout the Myst world and to eventually release the character which he or she believes to be innocent.

Setting:

The setting of Myst is unique and fantastic. "Myst" is an island in the middle of a forgotten sea. On this island is an odd assortment of objects and structures. There are forests, mountains, an ancient schooner, giant gears, a space vehicle, caves, craters, and other objects of curious origin. But the Myst island is only the beginning of the adventure. The Myst island is actually an island of keys and mysteries which allow the player to transport himself to the other "ages of Myst".

These "ages of Myst" are entire "worlds" which are centered around certain themes taken from the main Myst island.

- The Stoneship Age of Myst is the most ancient age. This age centers on the theme of a shipwrecked boat which has been inexplicably merged into a rocky island.

- The Mechanical Age of Myst is based on the theme of machines, gears, and a mysterious fortress of iron.

- The Channelwood Age of Myst is an island blanketed with gigantic trees and home to an abandoned city of tree-dwelling beings.

- The Selenitic Age of Myst is a dark age consisting of barren craters and volcanic underground caverns.

- In addition to these four primary ages of Myst, there are two smaller, hidden ages of Myst that play prominently at the conclusion of the game.

History of Myst:

The history of the Myst world (and the separate ages of Myst) is deep and rich. Much of this history will not be required knowledge of the player in the game. This history was developed to add depth and realism as well as consistency and continuity to the game play. The following narrative is a condensed version of Myst history:

Figure 3.3
Description and setting of *Myst* (image courtesy of Rand and Robyn Miller and Broderbund, 2005).

Long ago a masterful explorer set forth to discover worlds never dreamed of. After eons of adventures he grew tired of exploring known worlds and longed for the unknown. He perfected an art of writing that allowed him to produce fantastic books; these books were the doorways to other worlds. Through this art his exploring skills became unbound by the normal constraints of space and time. On an island he named "Myst," he built a library. In this library he housed the fruits of his labors: hundreds of books linking to the fantastic places and ages he had discovered.

Many years passed.

He sired two sons. As they grew, the explorer taught them about the power of the books and took them on great journeys. When they came of age, he gave them unbridled access to the library of Myst. The father's greatest pleasure was in listening to the many stories his sons would tell when they would return from their journeys. He had trusted them with his greatest treasure and they proved to be worthy of his trust. But time made him weary, and the stories made him sleep. The sons' travels soon went unsupervised. Slowly the riches and power of the journeys began to affect one of the sons. It began as simple greed; he would take from the Myst worlds more than he had brought. The evil grew; soon he gained pleasure from the conquest and destruction of the Myst worlds. To hide the abuse, he would mutilate the books linking to those worlds he had destroyed.

One day the father discovered the mutilation of the books and the corresponding devastation of the worlds. In a fit of rage, he imprisoned both sons within the pages of books designed to hold them until he could judge which of the sons was guilty (they both pleaded innocence). To discover the truth, he embarked on one final journey. He set out, only to perish along the way, leaving the sons entrapped forever.

His belongings were scattered far and wide, but his most important belonging, a single book, was one day discovered. This was the book that would allow him to return from his journey: the book of Myst. Without this book, no one would ever be able to visit the Island of Myst. Without this book, no one would ever be able finish the father's quest: judging the sons who still lay entrapped in their odd prisons.

The Game-play:

The Myst game-play is completely nonlinear. We will thus describe the game-play of Myst in a nonlinear fashion, relying on a series of maps, drawings, and illustrations. Obviously, we have simplified our descriptions, so as not to confuse anyone with unnecessary details. Our goal in this proposal is to communicate the Myst game-play in its simplest form.

The play begins with a view of an ancient book with the word "MYST" on its cover. When the player opens the book he is transported to the island of Myst with no explanations or directions whatsoever. He will find himself on the dock of the island...

Figure 3.4
History and gameplay of *Myst* (image courtesy of Rand and Robyn Miller and Broderbund, 2005).

Example   57

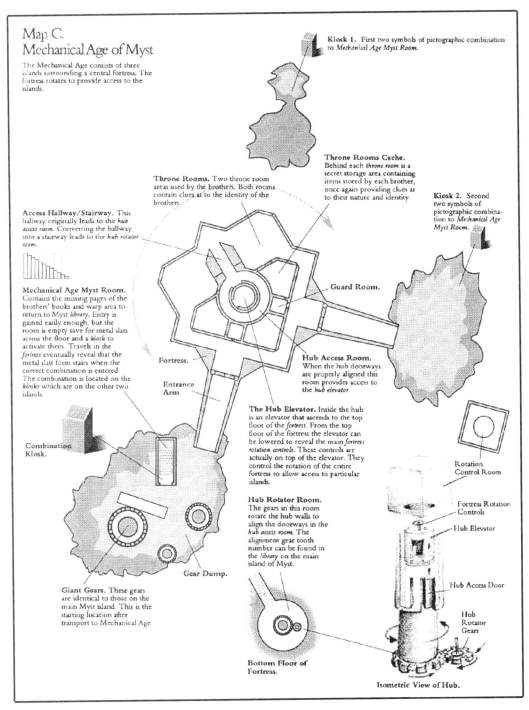

Map C.
Mechanical Age of Myst

The Mechanical Age consists of three islands surrounding a central fortress. The fortress rotates to provide access to the islands.

Kiosk 1. First two symbols of pictographic combination to *Mechanical Age Myst Room.*

Throne Rooms Cache. Behind each *throne room* is a secret storage area containing items stored by each brother, once again providing clues as to their nature and identity.

Throne Rooms. Two throne room areas used by the brothers. Both rooms contain clues as to the identity of the brothers.

Kiosk 2. Second two symbols of pictographic combination to *Mechanical Age Myst Room.*

Access Hallway/Stairway. This hallway originally leads to the *hub access room*. Converting the hallway into a stairway leads to the *hub rotator room*.

Mechanical Age Myst Room. Contains the missing pages of the brothers' books and warp area to return to Myst *library*. Entry is gained easily enough, but the room is empty save for metal slats across the floor and a *kiosk* to activate them. Travels in the *fortress* eventually reveal that the metal slats form stairs when the correct combination is entered. The combination is located on the *kiosks* which are on the other two islands.

Guard Room.

Fortress.

Entrance Arm

Hub Access Room. When the hub doorways are properly aligned this room provides access to the *hub elevator*.

The Hub Elevator. Inside the hub is an elevator that ascends to the top floor of the *fortress*. From the top floor of the fortress the elevator can be lowered to reveal the main *fortress rotation controls*. These controls are actually on top of the elevator. They control the rotation of the entire fortress to allow access to particular islands.

Rotation Control Room

Combination Kiosk.

Hub Rotator Room. The gears in this room rotate the hub walls to align the doorways in the *hub access room*. The alignment gear tooth number can be found in the *library* on the main island of Myst.

Fortress Rotation Controls

Hub Elevator

Gear Dump.

Giant Gears. These gears are identical to those on the main Myst island. This is the starting location after transport to Mechanical Age.

Hub Access Door

Hub Rotator Gears

Bottom Floor of Fortress.

Isometric View of Hub.

Figure 3.5
Mechanical Age of Myst map (image courtesy of Rand and Robyn Miller and Broderbund, 2005).

Review

In this chapter you should have learned the following:

- What a game design document (GDD) is and what goes in it.

- How to write a game design document.

- How to sell your game to a publisher through a proposal.

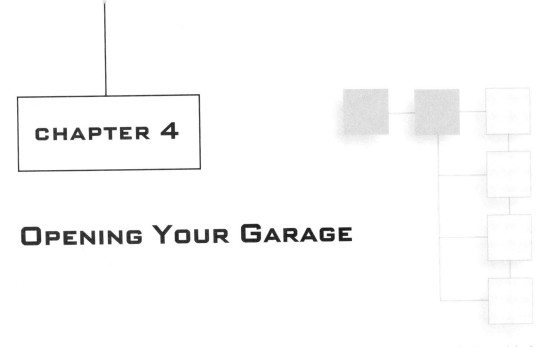

CHAPTER 4

OPENING YOUR GARAGE

Torque takes some patience to learn, but with a little practice and the added incentive that you will be building your very own game, you will become a Torque master. In this chapter, you will learn the basic Torque interface, before you move on to Chapter 5, "Wide Open Spaces," where we look at the Terrain Editor.

Jump-Starting Your Engine

Install the trial version of the Torque Game Engine SDK version 1.5 from the CD. It will add a shortcut to your Desktop, which will help you find the tools you need to run Torque every time. The Torque Game Engine SDK (Software Development Kit) will have the following shortcuts:

- **FPS Starter Kit**—This default mission runs a generic first person shooter game.

- **Racing Starter Kit**—This default mission runs a generic all-terrain racing game.

- **Torque Game Engine Demo**—This opens an introduction to what Torque is and what it is not.

- **Getting Started Tutorial**—This opens the basic tutorial for getting started using Torque, but if you're reading this book you'll get most of the documentation here.

- **Tutorial Base**—This opens the Torque WYSIWYG editors for the Getting Started Tutorial.

You will also find links to GarageGames, the online forums, software documentation, and the Torque Developer Network. We will not be using these in this book, but you might find them very useful. To look at the software documentation, you must be logged on to the GarageGames Web site, and then you will see general Torque documentation and Torque source code documentation.

Take Torque for a Test Drive

Open the Torque Game Engine Demo. You will be able to browse Torque's features (which we already covered in Chapter 2, "The Torque Game Engine") from the main panel. For now, you should click on the button to start the interactive walkthrough to see the engine's capabilities (see Figure 4.1).

As the engine loads, you may note that the loading bar goes slower when Lighting the Mission appears. This typically happens the first time a mission is loaded and is nothing to worry about. This can also happen when other people are playing your game.

When you see Welcome to Orc Town appear, follow the text and click on the arrow buttons at the bottom to peruse the many scenes, as they teach you about the game engine's special features one by one. There are several features, such as lighting, mirrors, and volumetric fog layers, which we've not covered before now. When you are finished, click on Exit and quit the demo.

When you are through with the interactive walkthrough, you may want to experience the FPS Starter Kit or the Racing Starter Kit. Each are designed to be all-in-one kits so that if you want to design a first-person shooter or racing game, you have most of the groundwork already laid out for you. Test out these game missions to experience what the player would see when playing them for the first time. These missions will also give you a preliminary impression of what the engine is capable of.

By now you are probably itching to get started developing in Torque. When you are ready, let's start.

Figure 4.1
Take the interactive walkthrough first.

Setting Up Your Work Environment

Your very first step is to set up a proper work environment. You must do this every time you start a new game project.

We will fudge by borrowing the initial FPS Starter Kit that comes with the Torque SDK. In the standard Torque file structure, the folder where the actual games are located is Torque\SDK\example. If you are using Windows, this will be on the C drive or whatever drive you installed Torque to. Find, copy, and paste a copy of the example folder into the same folder it is already in. Rename the copy of the example folder "experiment." This way we use the example folder and all its contents as our support code, but we still have a backup.

Open the experiment folder you just created, and you will see many folders and files within it. These are different example games. The starter.fps folder gives you all the source code and files you need for a first-person shooter. The starter.racing folder gives you the same for a racing game. The tutorial.base folder helps you through the Getting Started Tutorial to creating a freeform game.

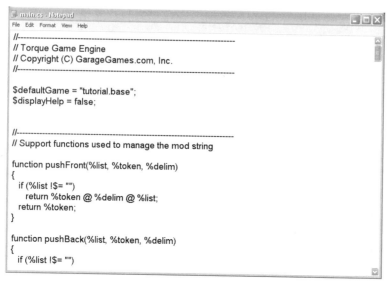

Figure 4.2
Opening main.cs in Notepad.

We are going to base our game on the starter.fps folder. Rename starter.fps as starter.yourname, putting your last name or handle where it says yourname.

The torqueDemo is the executable that will run your game. Rename the torque Demo executable YournameDemo, again using your surname or handle. In the same folder as YournameDemo, there will be a script file that is called main.cs. This is the first included script the Torque Game Engine looks for when it runs the executable. Open main.cs with a text editor on your computer (the most common text editor is Notepad, but use whatever you find available). Near the top you will see a line like this:

```
$defaultGame="tutorial.base";
```

This line (see Figure 4.2) tells the Torque engine where to look for the game's files. Change where it says tutorial.base to starter.yourname, being careful to leave the quotation marks where they're at. Also, this script is case sensitive so that means if you happen to have capitalized any letters when you renamed the folder, remember to capitalize them in the script. Then save the main.cs script file and exit.

Open the starter.yourname folder, and you'll see CS and CS.DSO files, as well as three other folders, including data, client, and server. The data folder contains the real meat and potatoes of your game, most especially the sound effects, texture files, 3D model files, and support scripts. The client and server folders share game

Figure 4.3
Your Start screen.

script content that we'll investigate later. The difference between CS and CS.DSO files is that CS.DSO files are compiled versions of the CS files, which speed the runtime of the engine. Whenever you run the game and the engine detects a change to a CS file, it will recompile the scripts and make a new CS.DSO file. It is good advice to delete old CS.DSO files after making changes to the CS files because CS.DSO files are sometimes read first by the engine, and the changes you made to the CS files could be ignored. Exit out of the starter.yourname folder and go back into the experiment folder.

Double-click (or single-click for Mac) to run YournameDemo. You should see the opening screen of the first-person shooter game (see Figure 4.3). When you are ready, press F11 to open the World Editor.

Getting Started in the World Editor

When you first open the World Editor, it will launch a new mission world, and you will see this world from a first-person camera mode (see Figure 4.4). The

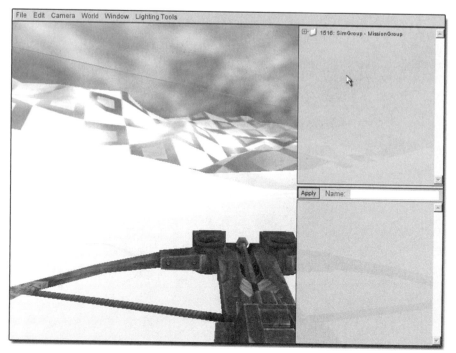

Figure 4.4
Resting on the ground plane after spawning.

panels to the right of your screen are the World Editor Inspector windows. You may not be able to see it, but a small gray square floating above the checkerboard terrain is where the player starts at, or the player *spawn point*. The spawn point is where the player character first appears in a level; in this instance, the player will start above the terrain and fall until he reaches the ground. You'll notice the blue bar on the player GUI goes down because it records lost stamina.

Movement

You start out in the player's perspective and can see the checkerboard from the player's point of view. If you can't, and if you are flying around in the air above your level, you are in camera-fly mode, and you'll have to camera toggle to get to the player's point of view. To do so, go to Camera > Toggle Camera. Use the default W, A, S, and D keys to walk around the checkerboard, and you can right-click and drag your mouse to look all around your current position. This mode of movement around the game world gives you an immediate feel for what the player will see and what the game experience will be like.

Later you can decide whether you want your game to be in first-person or third-person. You've experienced the first-person mode; now try out the third-person

File Edit Camera World Window Lighting Tools

Figure 4.5
Meet Korkins, the crazy orc guy from the Torque demo!

angle. You must right-click your mouse, then press the Tab key to switch to third-person perspective. The Inspector panels are going to get in your way. Turn them off for now by pressing F2 or going up to the menu bar and selecting Window > World Editor.

Walk around in third-person mode to get a feel for it. The default player model (see Figure 4.5) is the crazy Torque orc called Korkins. He even has his own Web site at korkins.com.

Let's go for the big picture. Go to Camera > Drop Camera at Player (or tap Alt+Q). You have left your body (eh, I mean the player model) behind and are floating around. Using the W, A, S, and D keys will allow you to move around in any direction, and you can still look around using the right mouse button. The camera may be too jumpy for adequate movement. If this is the case, you can change the camera speed by pressing the Shift key and any of the number keys between 1 and 7, 1 being the slowest and 7 being the most sensitive.

Look around the expanse of terrain for a while using the floating camera. If you get lost, you can always switch back to the first-person camera mode by pressing Alt+C or going to Camera > Toggle Camera.

Figure 4.6
Korkins is waiting for his close-up.

Using Drop Camera at Player (or free-floating mode, where you leave your model behind), scan the terrain until you see Korkins. At a distance, Korkins should be represented by a red square. Zoom in on Korkins until you see him onscreen. Notice that he is resting, or animating through his "idle" pose.

Selection

When you move your cursor over Korkins, it will change into a selection cursor to show you that he can be selected, and a green selection box shows which object will be selected (see Figure 4.6).

Click on Korkins, and a red bounding box and yellow bounding box appear (see Figure 4.7). The red box is supposed to be aligned to Korkins (or whatever object you have selected), while the yellow bounding box is aligned to the world he is set in. The yellow box will reveal what objects are selected as a group, and the red box will show what individual objects have been selected. Think of the red box as a "box within a box." Notice that if you pass your cursor over a selected object, such as Korkins here, the bounding box will turn blue.

Korkins (and just about every other object that winds up in your world) has a handle. This often appears as a number and name that float out beside the object they refer to. The number is set by where the objects lie in the object mission list and is also the server-side ID for the object, which will be important when you make an online game. The default name for objects is "null," which means it has no name.

Names are really optional, but you can assign names for objects to do some scripting. Go to Window > World Editor Inspector or press F3 to bring back the panels we previously got rid of. With Korkins selected, you should see all his information appear in the bottom half of the Inspector window (refer to Figure 4.7). There you should see an input field for name. Place your cursor in this field, type in **Korkins,** and then click the Apply button. On the screen, you will see Korkins' handle has changed to reflect his new name. Cool, huh?

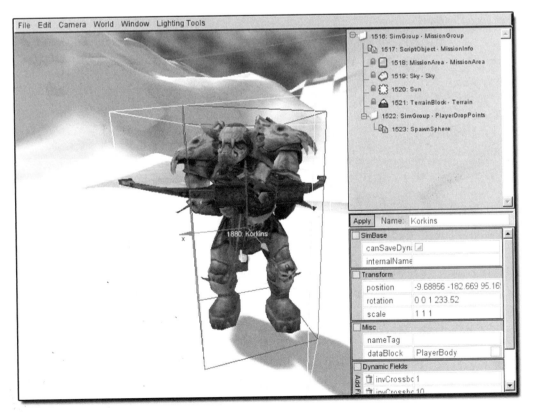

Figure 4.7
Giving Korkins a name for his handle.

Figure 4.8
The gizmo with handles for X, Y, and Z.

Manipulation

Korkins also has a gizmo that pops up when he's selected. The gizmo, as seen in Figure 4.8, is a three-handled device that should be fairly familiar to you if you have ever worked in a 3D program before. Each axis is used for a different direction in the virtual world. These handles give you the ability to move, rotate, and scale objects like Korkins here. When we say 3D, we mean that the world is three-dimensional, and in Torque these dimensions show up most prevalently as the Cartesian coordinate system that geometry buffs use. The Cartesian coordinate system plots paths and points on a grid using values X, Y, and Z, for left and right, forward and back, up and down.

To know how to use the gizmo, give it a whirl. However, you will have to learn some more hotkeys before you can manipulate objects.

Translate

To move Korkins around, simply right-click with your cursor on one of the handles X, Y, or Z and move him in that direction. Moving a 3D model is often called *translating*, so you will sometimes see a direction that tells you to translate an object. To translate means to move the object. Basic translation is object-dependent; if you want to translate along the world-axis, you have to hold down the Shift key. Notice that you can click and drag on Korkins without even using the gizmo, and he'll translate.

Rotate

To rotate Korkins from side to side on a central origin, click and hold the Alt key while clicking and dragging the Z axis handle (the blue bar) on the gizmo. You can make him spin around and do a 360 if you like.

Scale

To make Korkins bigger or smaller, look on the Inspector panel on the right under Transform > Scale. There are three coordinates: 1 1 1. Change the middle one to a 3, press the Apply button, and you'll have results similar to Figure 4.9.

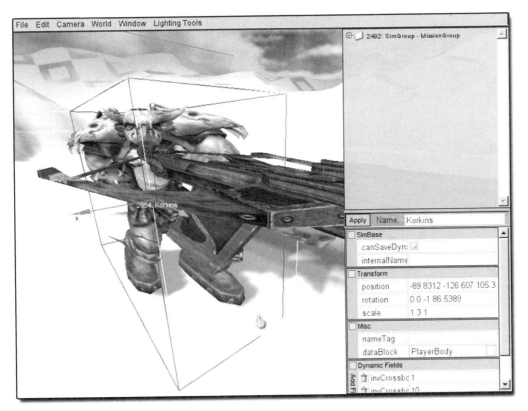

Figure 4.9
Stretching Korkins can be fun!

When you are done playing with Korkins, bring him back to normal by pressing Ctrl+Z (Win) or Cmd+Z (Mac) to undo your changes.

Manipulating with the World Editor Inspector

You could translate and rotate Korkins in the Inspector panel just as we did the scale, by entering values in the Inspector panel. In the bottom half of the Inspector panel, you have all of Korkins' data. Under the Transform section you should see values for position, rotation, and scale (refer to Figure 4.9). Each of these has a series of three digits beside it. These three digits reflect the X, Y, and Z axes of the object. You can change the values and click the Apply button to make them take effect.

Inspection

While you have the World Editor Inspector open, let's take a look at what it does. The Inspector allows you to manipulate a selected object via its script-based parameters, through text boxes, spinners, radio buttons, checkboxes, and more. These parameters vary based on the kind of object you select.

At the top of the Inspector you should see a World Editor tree, or list tree. Expand the list by clicking on the plus (+) sign next to the text ####: SimGroup - MissionGroup. The numbers vary slightly from one system to the next.

Figure 4.10
SimGroups.

SimGroups

SimGroups are similar to file folders in that they help you stay organized and make objects within SimGroups accessible for use with program scripts. You can have SimGroups within SimGroups, so they can be nested. In fact, everything in this scene is part of a big overall SimGroup called SimGroup - MissionGroup, as seen in Figure 4.10.

Review

In this chapter, you should have learned the following:

- What to do to set up your Torque workspace.

- How to start a new project using the basic examples.

- How to move your camera around inside the game world.

- How to select objects in the game world.

- How to transform objects you have selected in the game world (including translating, rotation, and scale).

- What the World Editor Inspector panel is for.

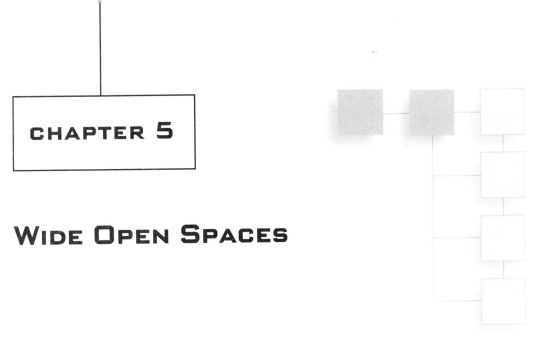

CHAPTER 5

WIDE OPEN SPACES

A lot of you may not find this to be work. It is a lot of work, but it's also like playing. If you used to enjoy playing with LEGOs or construction kits as a kid, or if you lost yourself in imaginary worlds of castles and kingdoms, you will find designing game worlds to be an exciting pastime that can make you money. Level designers create the environments that you move through and enjoy when playing video games. While the volume, complexity, and style of game levels may change between each game, designers use the same tried-and-true methods, architectural plans, and placement of obstacles to keep players consistently entertained and challenged.

We will look at what it takes to create game environments, what has been known to work before, and what you should keep in mind. Then you will build your first outdoor scene in the Torque Game Engine.

What a Game Level Is and Isn't

A large part of the game design document you draw up for your game will be composed of area maps and notes, and those are translated into game levels. A game level, whether it's a building interior or outdoor terrain, sets the stage for the achievement of gameplay.

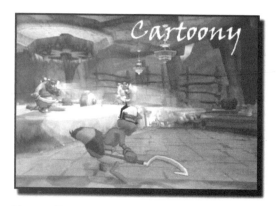

Figure 5.1
Cartoony versus realism (*Sly Cooper* and *Splinter Cell 3*, images courtesy of Sony, 2003 and Ubisoft, 2007, respectively).

A level designer has to make a level work in terms of fooling the player into believing that this image on the computer screen could be a real place and make it work as a stomping ground for the actions the player will take in it. Think of every game level you create as a movie set. Some of it will only have facades, or fake fronts. Some doors may lead to nowhere. Some elements may be incomplete. All that they have to do is operate on a psychological level to make the player think that she is somewhere you want her to think she is.

Levels often reflect the artistic choice for the game, so if you have a cartoony style, it would work to have cartoony game worlds; and if you are making a grungy spy thriller, you will more than likely have environments based on real places that are given a darker look (see Figure 5.1 for a comparison).

Level designers must also put landmarks in these environments. Landmarks are easily recognized "set pieces" that have unique enough features to keep players from wandering lost around the game world or from going around in circles. Landmarks can be anything (see Figure 5.2), as long as they stand out and get noticed.

A game level should do the following:

- Set the pace of game flow, including where resources and obstacles are laid.

- Fence the player in so she doesn't wander outside the main mission area.

- Act as a backdrop to the action that will take place.

- May be destructible or react in interesting ways to the player's actions.

- Tease the player with glimpses of a much wider world "out there."

Figure 5.2
One example of a landmark (*World of Warcraft*, image courtesy of Blizzard Entertainment, 2004–2007).

What a Level Designer Should Remember

The following are the best suggestions for you to keep in mind before developing a game world:

- Don't keep fiddling with a level. You should build it and move on. You can always edit later.

- Don't design a level so large that it becomes confusing and the player doesn't know where you want her to go next. Keep your levels small and tight.

- Don't place all your monsters, power-ups, and weapons in one single area. Spread them out and pace the game flow properly.

- Don't forget to give your player enough power-ups to survive but not so many that they make the game too easy.

- Don't make a game level so difficult it forms a "choke point" that frustrates the player. It can be easy to stump the player with puzzles, so be lenient.

- Like the theory behind feng shui, you should always keep the action in a game level moving.

- Try to accommodate all types of players, young and old, experienced and not so experienced.

- Always think of your game environment as an amusement park ride or a tourist vacation trap: you want to make it interesting, fun, and an escape away from the ordinary.

On that last point, think of yourself as an amusement tycoon. You must design for the player a place to come to, play, and leave with a sense of a unique experience. The more exciting the game world you design, the less likely players are to get bored playing your game. The more games you design, the more you will discover this to be true. No gamer has ever quit a game wishing it had been made less fun. As one reviewer said of Mario 64 after its release, "It was simply a lot of fun just running around, not really doing anything!"

Tip

"You want your game to be convincingly real to truly inspire mood and drama—and yet you have to be inventive, without straining credulity. It's a matter of combining and synthesizing, keeping the aspirations in your head, but looking for new ways to fit it all together."

—Marc Taro Holmes, Obsidian Entertainment

Exterior and Interior Spaces

In games, we have basically two kinds of spaces—exterior and interior.

Exterior spaces do not have a ceiling, not counting the sky. Exterior spaces allow the player to see for a great distance and to see more of the background (see Figure 5.3). Frequently, we use a type of exterior landscape geometry we call *terrain*. Terrain is organic, and it can appear very natural. Terrain can take the shape of rolling hills or steep mountains or cliff faces. Terrain can take up most of the real estate, with just a few buildings and other architecture for cover. In Torque, exteriors are made using the Terrain Editor and its sub-editors.

Interior spaces work differently from exterior spaces. In video games, an interior space is any space that is indoors and has a ceiling (see Figure 5.4). Interiors are

Figure 5.3
An exterior space (*Galleon*, image courtesy of Atlus USA, 2004).

Figure 5.4
An interior space (*Max Payne*, image courtesy of Rockstar Games, 2001).

often smaller, man-made instead of organic, and typically have more visible detail because they cause less strain on the computer memory resources. Interiors are created separately from exteriors and brought into the World Editor. Interiors are DIF files built in Torque Constructor, QuArK, or another map editor. We'll look at creating interiors specifically in Chapter 6, "Interior Design Isn't for Decorators."

Under the Hood of the Terrain Editor

We're going to use Torque's GeoTerrain tools to get a hands-on feel for sculpting and manipulating terrain. Start up YournameDemo from the executable. Start up a new mission by pressing F11. Then press the F6 key or go to Window > Terrain Editor. Select Camera > Toggle Camera to make sure you're up in the air, looking down at the lay of the land from a free-floating camera view.

Terrain Editor Display

You might not see a whole lot of difference between the World Editor and Terrain Editor at first, except that you won't have the Inspector panels obscuring your view. You'll also notice that wherever you move your cursor, a bunch of little colored squares follow it around, as in Figure 5.5. These colored squares reflect the size, shape, and type of brush you have selected, and your brush will affect the terrain when you start clicking.

Click-drag somewhere on the terrain to see what I mean. When you have made a tiny hill, you can use Ctrl+Z (Win) or Cmd+Z (Mac) to go back.

There are two other displays at the bottom of your screen: Mouse Brush and Selection.

- **Mouse Brush**—This scale shows how many vertices, or tiny points, are currently under the brush, and it shows the average elevation of the vertices.

- **Selection**—This scale tells you how many vertices you have selected and the average elevation of these vertices.

The Brush

You can change brush size by going up to Brush on the menu and choosing one of the other brush sizes. The Terrain Editor always seems to default to 9 × 9 units,

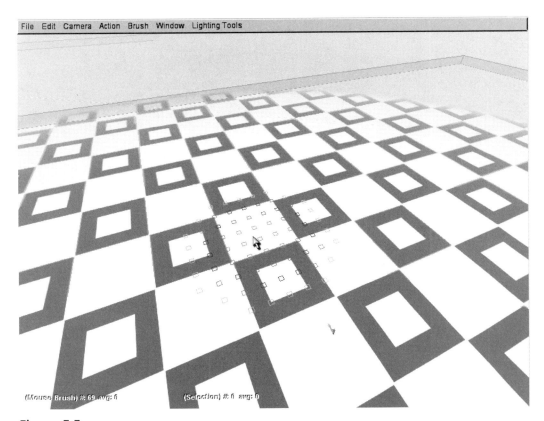

File Edit Camera Action Brush Window Lighting Tools

(Mouse Brush) # 69 avg: 0   (Selection) # 0 avg: 0

Figure 5.5
The default brush area.

but you have the option of sizes 1×1 units up to 25×25 units. As you can see, changing the brush size affects the number of red and green squares you have following your mouse around.

Red squares indicate areas that will be most affected in terms of relative influence, and green squares indicate areas that will be least affected or almost neutral. Red squares have 100% influence, thus they move more when you click-drag than other colored squares. You may, during the course of construction, see orange and yellow squares. In terms of relative hardness, these squares are as follows:

- **Red**—100% influence

- **Orange**—More than 50% influence

- **Yellow**—Less than 50% influence

- **Green**—Almost 0% influence, or totally neutral

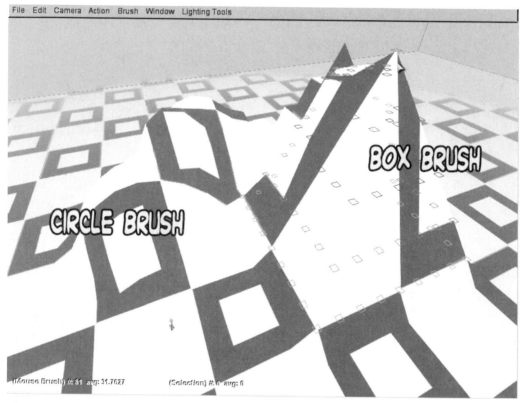

File Edit Camera Action Brush Window Lighting Tools

BOX BRUSH

CIRCLE BRUSH

(Mouse Brush) # 81 avg: 31.7627   (Selection) # 0 avg: 0

Figure 5.6
The difference in working with a box or circle brush.

If you select Brush > Soft Brush, you have the variable strength pattern across the brush as depicted above. If you select Brush > Hard Brush, the brush acts at 100% hard (all red squares) across the entire brush area.

You can also change the shape of the brush from a circle to a box (see Figure 5.6). If you want to make a hard wall or cliff face out of the terrain, you should use a hard brush set to a box shape. Otherwise, the most organic brush to use would be a soft brush set to a circle.

Actions

On the menu, open up Action. You will see that there are several basic brush actions available. The default action is set to Adjust Height.

You can choose Add Dirt, which raises the terrain under the brush wherever you click. This is good for creating mounds, hills, mountains, peaks, cliffs, and even walls. You can also choose Excavate, which lowers the terrain under your brush and can be very good for constructing valleys and pits.

When working closely on hills and valleys using Add Dirt or Excavate, you may end up with serious demarcated lines between them. If this happens, just use the Smooth action, which averages vertices between the nearest neighbors to where you place your brush.

Another popular action you can use is Flatten, which sets all the terrain underneath the brush to the average height of the vertices. (You can see the average height of vertices under the brush at any time by looking at the Mouse display at the bottom of your screen.) Flatten is useful for creating plateaus and man-made platforms. This is what I will use when creating the flat even plateaus on our map, which I'm about to show you.

Making Ravenscroft

Your first game that you construct in the Torque Game Engine will be a first-person shooter. It is called *Abandon All Hope*.

The Game We'll Make

Name: *Abandon All Hope* (see Figure 5.7)

Genre: First-person shooter

Figure 5.7
Abandon All Hope.

Style: Dark comedy

Player Character: Little Reaper

Setting: A spooky churchyard and village called Ravenscroft.

Synopsis: The player is Little Reaper, a short cartoony image of Death, and he must run around Ravenscroft and catch as many Skulls as time permits to get the highest score. There are also obstacles for him to avoid.

Go ahead and use the movement and Terrain Editor skills you've learned to create the sort of terrain you see in the churchyard map (see Figure 5.8). This is going to be the main level you create for your first 3D game in Torque.

You should start with a square brush at 100% influence and click-drag to pull up the levels of height you need. The exact size and height will be different for everybody. If you feel like your island is getting too large, that's fine; but if you feel like your island is too small or cramped when you switch back to the player's point of view, then make it bigger. After making large plateau steps, you should switch to a round brush with a graduated influence and click-drag to pull the sides of the island up. Of course, incongruities will appear. Use a combination of

Figure 5.8
Churchyard map.

the Flatten and Smooth brush commands to sculpt the main mass of the island into a decent structure.

If you make a mistake, don't hesitate; remember that most of the time you can go back by pressing Ctrl+Z (Win) or Cmd+Z (Mac). You can iron out a mistake if it's on the terrain usually by switching brush actions. Keep your construction loose and organic, without making it look too rigid or man-made. Save often, as sometimes the Undo command does not work. When you save, save as YournameDemoMission.mis in YournameDemo\data\missions.

You're going to start by making the entire Ravenscroft land hump like a hill; we'll fill the valley around it with water in the next section, but prepare the edge of Ravenscroft to be an island. Then fill in the other details around the churchyard. Make plateaus where you know that you'll place buildings later on, and you won't have as much trouble then.

Tip

> If you have altered the terrain in such a way that the player's character winds up beneath the terrain, you will have to toggle on the camera, move the camera to a place well above the terrain, and then select Camera > Drop Player at Camera (Alt+W). Your player will wind up wherever you moved your camera to and above the terrain instead of under it.

Water

Somewhat complicated, water has gotten a lot of attention on the community forums. Programmers are best at simulating water in Torque. Water is an environmental product that already comes as part of the Torque Game Engine, yet it certainly looks and acts better if scripted from scratch. But I bet you probably don't want to code water from scratch this early on, do you?

The following is the surest method for creating a water block in Torque. Water is supposed to be a liquid, you might be thinking, so why do I call it a "water block"? In 3D worlds, designers create cubes and apply water effects to them. These cubes then get sunk into the world terrain so that you just see their surfaces. That way you don't have to model the interior contours of the water shape, which would end up being a long haphazard affair.

Insert a new water block by going to Window > World Editor Creator (or press F4). From the list on the right, expand Mission Objects and expand Environment until you see a list of prefabricated environment objects. Click on Water. You don't have to give the water block a name; just click OK in the pop-up window to exit it (see Figure 5.9).

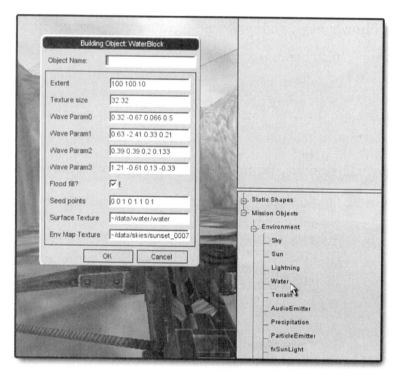

Figure 5.9
Adding a water block in Torque.

You now have a water block, but we have to adjust its attributes to make it work right. Enter the World Editor Inspector by hitting F3. Find your water block and click on it to select it. Its attributes will appear on the right. Scroll down to find the Media section, and change its SurfaceTexture to YournameDemo\data\water\water.png. Under the Debugging section, you should click on the checkbox next to UseDepthMask to remove the gray hash mark. Under Surface, you must change envMapIntensity to 0.0.

Notice that in the Surface section, there's also an attribute called surfaceOpacity, as in Figure 5.10. It defaults to 0.75, which is great because that means it will be slightly transparent, or 75% opaque.

That's it! Stretch out your water block really big and put it where you need it, preferably down low so it covers up only part of the terrain and makes Ravenscroft into an island. I had trouble scaling my water block correctly, so here's what I did: under the water block's attributes, in the Transform section, is a place for Scale. I set the numbers at 500 500 10, which makes it 10 units tall and 500 units wide in both directions. Depending on the size of your island, you

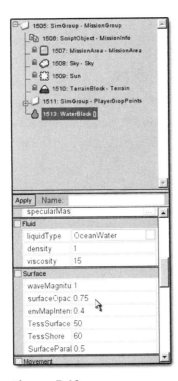

Figure 5.10
The attributes of the water block.

might want to go even bigger. Hit Apply and then select Toggle Camera to preview it.

Relighting Your World

When you're satisfied with the look of your churchyard, go to Lighting Tools > Full Relight to update all the lights in your level. Relighting is done on the fly when your scene is loaded into the editor, but when you change the terrain in the Terrain Editor you must manually relight the scene so that you can see the updates without having to reload the scene from the start. Typically, you will want to relight a scene after you think you are through building the terrain.

Once the scene has been relit, go to Camera > Toggle Camera and strut about your newly developed churchyard to see everything from the player's point of view.

Saving Your Mission

You've done a fair bit of building so far, so it's a good idea to pause and save your game. To do so, select File > Save Mission As and choose YournameDemo\data\missions, and therein save your project as YournameDemoMission.mis.

The Terrain Texture Painter

Let's set up our textures. On the CD, look in projects\churchyard\textures. Copy and paste these texture files to YournameDemo\data\terrains. When it prompts you to overwrite existing files, tell it yes.

With YournameDemoMission.mis open, go to Window > Terrain Texture Painter.

Terrain painting is pretty fun and straightforward. You should see a palette of six texture options on the right of the screen. The palette has default textures, but you can place others in it by clicking on the Add or Change buttons. If you click the Add or Change buttons, a Load File window will open up (see Figure 5.11). You can use two different image file types, JPEG or PNG, but they have to be some factor of 8 × 8 pixels, like 64 × 64 or 256 × 256.

You can have eight textures in Torque, but the editor restricts you to six. This actually saves rendering time at 800 × 600 resolutions, and it is recommended that you stay within this parameter. However, if you feel you absolutely must have more than that number of textures, you can search the GarageGames Web site for a topic titled "8 Terrain Textures Instead of 6"

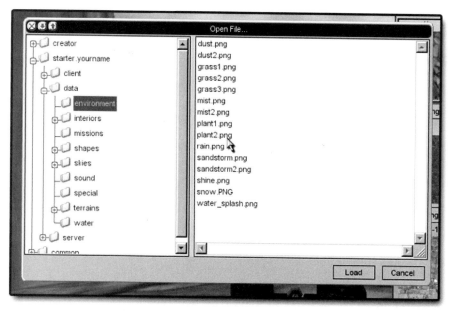

Figure 5.11
Adding or changing textures.

to find a patch that will get you more (warning: it will involve some additional coding).

Right now, click the Change button under the checkerboard texture. On the left, you'll see a tree of available folders. Click on YournameDemo and find data and terrains. Look for the ground1 texture, and then click OK. You'll see a dramatic difference when you're back in the Editor window. Everything that was painted with a checkerboard is now painted with a jazzy ground1 texture.

There's only one other texture that will suit our designs, and it is grass, so click the Add button on the square beneath the ground1 you just did. You should use these textures (see Figure 5.12) to paint the churchyard terrain. Go right ahead and use the grass.jpg to paint highlights over your mounds and terrain features. Notice how areas where you brush blend into adjacent areas really well. If you mess up on anything, don't fret if the Undo command doesn't work; you can always paint it back out.

Figure 5.12
Textures loaded into the palette.

Figure 5.13
The churchyard after you've painted it.

When you are through painting your churchyard, your work should look similar to Figure 5.13. Go ahead and walk around it in the player perspective (Camera > Toggle Camera) to get a feel for it. Also see if you missed a spot or if there is anything else to be added. You don't need to relight your scene after painting textures on it, only when you reshape it. Save your mission and exit.

Make Your Own Textures

Textures are used to enhance the 3D game environment, pure and simple. The proper use of textures can also convey a mood or feeling, as well as establish a time and place. You can get textures from almost anywhere.

Many game developers actually use digital cameras to take close-up photos of buildings, walls, drainage pipes, metal grills, and more. If you don't have a digital camera, which can plug right into your computer, you can use a basic film camera and scan in images. Scanners are pretty low-cost items these days. When you do find a perfect candidate to use as a texture, remember to snap shots of it from as many angles, distances, and lighting situations as possible.

Besides using photos, you can draw or paint your own textures using traditional media, such as oil paints, pastels, or other. Or you can go all high-tech and create your textures inside the paint software program of your choosing. There are several plug-in brushes for Adobe Photoshop, for instance, you can download that are very useful for creating random rough surface textures.

One matter to always bear in mind when getting textures is that they have to balance well with the other textures you are going to use for your game. The lighting, color contrast, and shape have to be a fairly decent match and coordinate well when stuck on 3D objects in a game level.

Textures are also meant to be tiled. Say that you found a great image of some rough patch of ground. If you do nothing to it and try to use it in Torque, you might see some hard edges where the texture meets up with itself and doesn't blend very well. If this happens, there is a straightforward process you can use to make the image tile properly. This technique works with all paint packages, including Adobe Photoshop or an open-source program, such as Gimp or Paint Dot Net.

Let's try it now. On the CD in projects\Chapter 5, there's an image file called bricks. jpg. Open it into your paint program. If you don't have a paint program that you use on your computer, might I suggest Paint Dot Net, which is available on the CD.

Drag your marquee selection tool over the left-most edge, as in Figure 5.14. You're going to mirror the sides to their opposite edges. So with this small edge on the left, copy it and horizontally flip its duplicate copy over to the right side. Do the same with the bottom edge up to the top edge using a vertical flip. After you place these duplicated edges, you're going to have to merge them with the underlying layers and spend some time getting them to blend well with the original. The more complicated the pattern on the texture, the more work you'll have to do to keep the entire image consistent.

When you're done, your image should look similar to Figure 5.15. Save it as bricks_final.jpg in YournameDemo\data\terrains.

Launch YournameDemo and get into the Terrain Editor. Open the Terrain Texture Painter and pick one of the slots, selecting the Change button and finding bricks_final.jpg in YournameDemo\data\terrains. Use your brush to paint the

Figure 5.14
You're going to duplicate this edge.

Figure 5.15
Your final bricks texture.

Figure 5.16
How your bricks texture looks when applied.

terrain with it and see if it tiles nicely or not. It should come out like Figure 5.16. You might not want to mess up your pretty terrain, so paint over the bricks if you like.

Broken Textures

If you ever reload or relight your scene, and you see all-white terrain or textures seemed to have disappeared on you, then what you have are broken file paths. To fix this, follow these steps:

1. Open the Terrain Texture Painter (Window > Terrain Texture Painter).

2. If you see blank texture slots, but they have the appropriate names beneath them, you know you have broken file paths.

3. One by one, click Change and relocate the original textures by browsing your machine for them.

4. Finally, save the terrain, and your terrain's textures should be fixed.

Detail Textures

When walking around in your churchyard, you have probably realized that the terrain's textures look pretty cool when far away, but when you get up close and personal with the ground, it looks pretty weird, even grainy. This is because when you are close up to the terrain, the textures become magnified. You can fix this with adding detail textures.

We'll do the ground detail texture to get you started, since it encompasses a pretty large tract of land here. Open up the World Editor Inspector (Window > World Editor Inspector) and select TerrainBlock - Terrain from the Mission-Group in the list tree.

You should see terrain data pop up in the bottom half of the Inspector window. Under Media, find detailTexture and click on the browse button (. . .) beside it. Browse until you find YournameDemo\data\terrains\detail1.png (which you should have copied off the CD when you copied the textures). Load it.

Take another look at the ground. Get real close, and you will see a vast improvement in its appearance, as shown in Figure 5.17. How does it do that, you might ask? The engine uses something called FOV (field of view) and checks the distance from the player's line of sight and the textured terrain to overlay textures on the fly in order to incorporate more detail without overtaxing the computer's memory space. When you are done experimenting, save your mission and move on.

Pimp My Torque: Advanced Tips

There are other ways to make terrain besides the direct sculpting and manipulation technique as stated previously, and there are also several ways to improve your terrain once you've built it and painted it.

Terrain Height-Maps

Not all the ways to create terrain in Torque are as nearly as hands-on as the direct sculpting method. One of these other methods is to use height-maps, which we'll look at here.

The concept of height-maps is so elegant it appears fascinatingly simple. You can create a flat 2D image, usually a PNG file, which is just like a topological

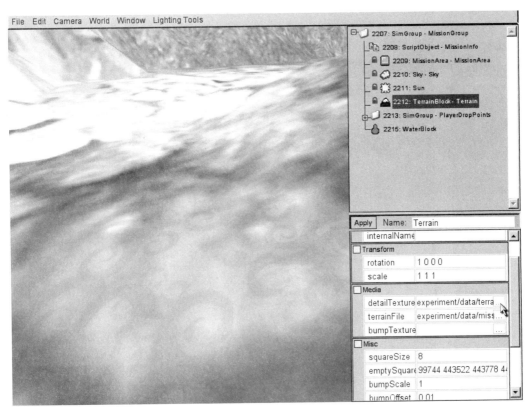

File   Edit   Camera   World   Window   Lighting Tools

2207: SimGroup - MissionGroup
  2208: ScriptObject - MissionInfo
  2209: MissionArea - MissionArea
  2210: Sky - Sky
  2211: Sun
  2212: TerrainBlock - Terrain
  2213: SimGroup - PlayerDropPoints
  2215: WaterBlock

Apply | Name: Terrain

	internalName
Transform	
rotation	1 0 0 0
scale	1 1 1
Media	
detailTexture	experiment/data/terra...
terrainFile	experiment/data/miss...
bumpTexture	
Misc	
squareSize	8
emptySquare	99744 443522 443778 44
bumpScale	1
bumpOffset	0.01

Figure 5.17
A close-up view of a detail texture.

map of the terrain. Then you import it into a modeling program as a "height-map" (many 3D modeling programs offer this), and the modeling program will create a terrain object based on it, which can then be textured before it is brought into Torque and stretched, rotated, and moved around in place. The way the modeling program processes the height-map is by variances in light and dark. The darkest areas of the PNG file become the pits and valleys, and the lightest areas become the peaks and hilltops. Look at Figure 5.18 as an example of before and after.

This can be a fun process for many game developers, but as Torque allows for terrain manipulation and editing right inside the engine itself and is easier to edit on the fly, height-maps have not been mentioned.

For creating height-maps using Milkshape 3D, look at Kenneth C. Finney's book *3D Game Programming All In One* (Course Technology PTR, 2006).

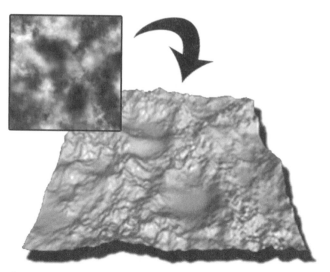

Figure 5.18
A height-map in action.

Climate and Terrain Special Effects

You can add specific weather, layers of fog, and even change the look of the sky to enhance your game levels. These are all popular ways game designers make their levels look unique and realistic.

Weather

A couple of really nice effects that Torque comes with are precipitation and lightning. These are separate mission objects you can add to your scene, and they are found in the World Editor Creator (F4). On the list on the right, press the plus sign out beside it to expand Mission Objects and then do the same for Environment. You'll see a list of prefabricated objects Torque is set to handle. The only drawback to these objects is that most of them take some scripting, depending on the prototype you're using.

The following are the most commonly used objects by garage game designers:

- **Precipitation**—Precipitation can appear as rain, snow, or more, and is represented by image files with multiple billboard sprites on them and attributes you have to set for velocity and collision.

- **Lightning**—The engine generates random jagged lightning bolts that strike the terrain at intervals. One really neat fact is that you can (to some degree) tell the engine where the lightning should strike.

Figure 5.19
Ever-present fog of *Silent Hill 2* (image courtesy of Konami, 2000).

- **Thunder/Textured Lightning**—Sometimes you'll see features of thunder or textured lightning. These can enhance the effect of a simulated storm.

You can look online to find forum threads covering the addition of these effects.

Fog

Since the creation of the spooky horror game *Silent Hill*, fog has played an important addition in games (see Figure 5.19). Fog appears in Torque as general fog, and you have access to up to three fog layers. I won't have you mess with fog for your *Abandon All Hope* game, but I will tell you a little something about it.

The first type of fog—general fog—affects visibility in the level no matter where you are, and it is controlled by the fogDistance attribute. Low fogDistance values represent low visibility, and high values represent better visibility.

Volumetric fog is a three-dimensional effect that fakes realistic fog environments. The layered fog, a type of volumetric fog, appears in actual layers. You can move layered fog into a level to complement moving clouds in the background, to settle in low-lying valleys, or for the inside of water blocks (to give underwater areas a murky appearance).

Just to show you what you're looking for, in the YournameDemo\data\missions folder there's a mission (MIS) file stronghold.mis. Just for giggles, open this file in Notepad or other text editor you use for coding. You will notice the new Sky(Sky) block settings starting with the word "fog." The ones you want to pay attention to are

```
fogVolume1 = "0 0 0";
fogVolume2 = "0 0 0";
fogVolume3 = "0 0 0";
```

This code snippet sets layered fog for each new mission. The parameters, from left to right, after the volume label, are distance, bottom level, and top level. What it means after fogVolume1 is that the first layer will start at 0 world units and stop at 0 world units, with a visible distance of 0 world units.

Skybox

Remember that sky you see in Torque (and in most of the electronic games you play)? It's a box. Designers call these *skyboxes*. Basically a skybox has six sides with pictures on them that render in the engine as a dome that covers the virtual world. In Torque, the Sky object you see in the Inspector list renders as a skybox. In addition to the six sides of the box, you also have three cloud layers that animate by moving across the sky and three fog layers, which we've already looked at.

Open up YournameDemo\data\skies folder, and you'll see the texture files with the DML (material list) file tucked inside. This DML file specifies your skybox texture files and cloud texture files.

The quickest way to replace the sky that your game reveals is to create a new skies folder with a similar material list and point to the material list in the World Editor Inspector. This can be complicated, however, as you have to be very careful about lining up each texture so they tile really well together. Make sure to save backups of all your files, just in case you make a mistake.

If you try to make the sky look like it's nighttime, you can replace the sky textures, but you'll still have a sun in your sky. You cannot delete the sun altogether or your game will crash, unless you're using the Torque Lighting Kit. Instead, select Sun in the Inspector, and set its color and ambient color parameters to 0 0 0 0 (or pure black).

Tip

The Sun object in your world controls the virtual sun's placement. Its placement is based on elevation (how high the sun is in the skybox) and azimuth (compass direction). Elevation is usually set at 45 degrees, and at 90 degrees the engine will crash. Azimuth can be set at 0 to 360 degrees (at 90 or 180 degrees shadows will not render in the scene).

Copy and paste the projects\churchyard\skies folder to YournameDemo\data, overwriting your original skies folder. Then, with your mission open, click F3 to go to the World Editor Inspector. Click on Sky - Sky in the tree list on the top right to bring up the current sky's attributes on the bottom right. Find the Media section, and click on the browse button beside MaterialList. Expand the list beside YournameDemo and data and select skies.

There should be a DML file inside called sky_day.dml, which you should select. Click Load. Voilà—you now have a totally different and cartoonier sky! See Figure 5.20.

Figure 5.20
A change of sky, and a breath of fresh air.

Q & A with Dylan Romero of GarageGames

What was Torque based on? What formed its origins?

"When GarageGames was formed, an engine was needed to build games and tools on. Since the founders of the company had worked extensively on *Tribes 2*, they decided to use the code behind that game to form the first iteration of the Torque engine."

Who can use Torque? Is it best for programmers, artists, designers, or students?

"Torque is best used by a team consisting of programmers, artists, and designers, because all these skills are necessary to create a great game—even if that game is created by a 'team' of just one person. Students are of course included in this summary. As long as you have the skills, you can create a game using Torque. DeVry, ITT Tech, Brown, Michigan State University, and many other colleges and tech schools use Torque in the classroom as a useful tool for learning game development."

What game genres are best to develop using Torque? Are there any limits?

"Torque was initially made for *Tribes 2*, so first-person shooters are obviously one of the genres Torque supports. Since its release, however, nearly every game genre has been created using Torque. Platformers, MMOs, fighting games, RTSs, puzzle games . . . all of them have been created using the Torque engine. Tweaking of the source code might be necessary to create certain aspects of gameplay, but the engine itself provides almost everything a developer needs."

What is the youngest age of a developer using Torque to date, and what have they created?

"Many teens own a copy of Torque, the youngest of which I know about is 14 years old."

What has been the most popular best-selling game using Torque in recent years?

"The *Marble Blast* series has easily been the most popular GarageGames-developed Torque title in recent years, thanks in part to its success on Xbox Live Arcade. It still sells very well to this day."

To someone just starting out in game design, what would be your most important advice to them?

"Start small. Many people never finish projects because they want to create something like a Halo-killer or an MMORPG right off the bat. Finishing a relatively modest project will give you a realistic idea of what problems and challenges can spring up during the course of creating a game. The last 10% of any project is the hardest to complete."

What can we see in Torque's future? Where will GarageGames take it next?

"Torque has branched off into many directions. While TGE continues development, new engines such as TGEA, TGB, and Torque X have filled in the development gaps forming a suite of affordable engines covering the needs of both hobbyists and AAA game developers. The future of Torque lies in bringing all these tools together into one simple solution for anyone looking to make a game using accessible yet powerful game technology."

What's Next?

That pretty much concludes our look at outdoor environments for games. Next we'll peek at creating indoor environments, using the Torque Constructor. The principles for game level design stay the same, no matter what editor or engine

Figure 5.21
You can make all kinds of outdoor scenes now, including this one!

you use. What you've learned you can apply to all kinds of different games when it comes to designing levels. So scale those peaks (as in Figure 5.21), and you'll be surprised what you find for yourself!

Review

After reading this chapter, you should know the following:

- How to make great game levels and what goes into level design.

- What the difference is between interior and exterior 3D spaces.

- How to open the Terrain Editor.

- How to sculpt terrain using the brush.

- How to change the brush you work with.

- How to paint textures directly to the terrain.

- How to make your own textures to paint with.

- How to fix broken texture file paths.

- How to add detail textures for a refined look.

- What height-maps are and how they can be used to create terrain.

- How to add weather, water blocks, and fog into your levels.

- How to change the look of the default sky in Torque.

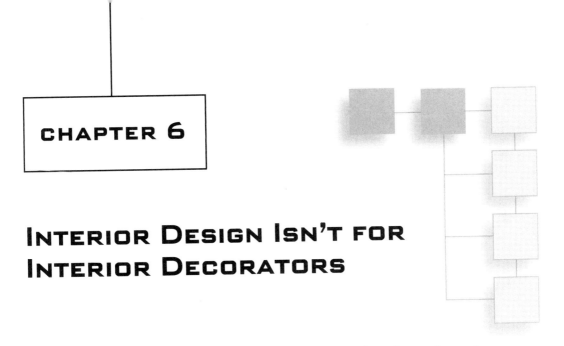

CHAPTER 6

INTERIOR DESIGN ISN'T FOR INTERIOR DECORATORS

In the last chapter, we made the distinction between interior and exterior spaces. We focused on outdoor, or exterior, environments in that chapter. This chapter is just the opposite. We'll be going inside and creating indoor environments and other structures for use in Torque. The way we do this is through the construction of DIF files.

What's the DIF?

DIF files are the heart and soul of CSG-built structures. DIF files can have complex shapes, light maps, and collision surfaces, and they don't get animated. DIF files use portals for their rendering, and these portals are useful for culling visibility, which means that if the player can't directly see parts of objects or rooms, the rendering engine doesn't draw them.

This chapter will be about making DIF files; the next one, Chapter 7, "This Isn't the Runway: Modeling 101," will cover DTS creation. Torque makes animation easy with DTS files. However, DTS files are not recommended for buildings and other large structures (like the rooms of a haunted house, as seen in Figure 6.1). The DIF format is much better suited for this purpose, as it provides more efficient culling of off-screen geometry and for more precise collision. Before you go any farther, you should understand the difference between DTS and DIF. For an allegory that most of you science-fiction types would understand, DTS files are like sleek space cruisers, and DIFs are like cargo ships. The space cruisers are

Figure 6.1
These rooms should be built mostly from DIF files.

made to get up and go and don't stop for anything. The cargo ships are larger, more lumbering, and often get used as sets for exploration missions where travelers find nasty alien invaders on board.

DIFs are created with CSG modeling. When you're all through constructing a scene in the Torque Constructor, QuArK, or other CSG editor, you must compile the scene as a DIF for use in Torque.

CSG Modeling

CSG stands for Constructive Solid Geometry, and the concept behind CSG modeling is a little different from that of polygon modeling. With CSG, you build things out of brushes. Imagine that brushes are like building blocks. You pick a building block, like the cylinder, and construct with it. A cylinder's not the only building block for you to choose from; in many CSG editors, there are also cubes, cones, ramps, and occasionally spheres or arches. You build with these brushes in one of three different ways. You can intersect them, join them, or subtract with them. (In the last case, the brush actually acts as a giant eraser!)

CSG modeling is not just for constructing indoor maps, however. CSG modeling can be used to create any complex structure with collision surfaces. Therefore, many designers refrain from calling CSG constructs "interiors." If you want to develop objects that characters can walk on or around in, they have to be CSG, but you will not be able to create these spaces in 3ds Max or other modeling tools. CSG editing, therefore, is a necessary skill to learn.

Note

The Torque Constructor is not the only CSG editor out there. As I've mentioned, QuArK has been used by developers since before Constructor was ever developed, but beginners can find QuArK difficult to set up and learn how to use. For the sake of continuity here, I'll focus on the Torque Constructor in the following tutorials.

DIF Creation Software

There are several tools you can use to do CSG modeling and make DIFs for Torque, not just the Torque Constructor, which we'll get to in just a moment. All of the following DIF creation software programs must be purchased separately and require the 2004 map2dif conversion plug-in (found on the CD in the software folder).

QuArK

Cartography Shop 4.0

Radiant

Max2map (a separate plug-in for 3D Studio Max)

Game Level Builder

Caligari GameSpace

Blender

Maya Level Tools 5.0

Except for QuArK and the Torque Constructor, none of these programs are supported by GarageGames nor are they fully tested. Most of them have limited use. That is why we will use the Torque Constructor, which GarageGames provides free, and you can find it in the CD's software folder for installation. Price-wise, free is good!

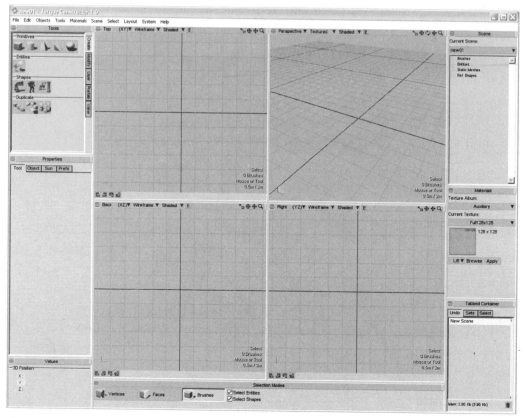

Figure 6.2
Torque Constructor.

Under the Hood of the Torque Constructor

Torque Constructor (see Figure 6.2) is a solid cross-platform CSG editor that supports numerous industry-standard model formats. Because it's the brainchild of GarageGames' Matt Fairfax, Tom Brampton, John Kabus, Dave Wyand, and Ron Yacketta, Torque Constructor can also seamlessly export into the Torque Game Engine (TGE) or Torque Game Engine Advanced (TGEA).

Features

Torque Constructor's main features include the following:

- Basic brushes (Cube, Cylinder, Sphere, Pyramid, and Ramp)

- User-scriptable custom tools

- CSG subtraction, intersection, knife, slice, and clip

- The ability to hide, lock, and edit selections for more precise control

- Face and vertex editing

- Concave brush detection

- Export and import prefabricated shapes

- Duplication and cloning tools

Everything you create in Constructor is called a *scene*. A scene, by GarageGames' definition, is a collection of 3D objects. Constructor may call them scenes, but you may also hear them referred to as rooms or maps, based on the design background of the game level artists making them. The Constructor scene's native format is CSX, but you will want to save your scenes as MAP files so that you can transfer them to DIF later. MAP files are standard fair in the CSG world.

Build a Crate

If you haven't done so already, install Torque Constructor from the CD. You're going to make a crate—because every game ever made has had crates in some form or another in them somewhere.

Making a Crate

Once installed, launch Torque Constructor. In the upper-left corner, you'll see the Tools form, as shown in Figure 6.3. It's the one with tabs for Create, Modify,

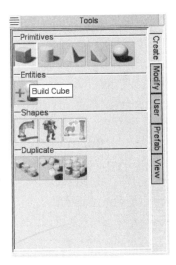

Figure 6.3
The Tools form.

User, Prefab, and View down its right side. Under Primitives at the top, you should click on the cube shape. You've just selected the cube to be your brush. Your brush icon and your cursor will change to reflect this.

Position your cursor over the Top view pane (which is the upper-left corner of the four Constructor window panes). These panes all show you the exact same 3D area, but from different angles.

Let me digress for just a moment so you will understand what these window panes do. Imagine for a second that the object you're trying to make is inside a shoebox with a lid on it. You want to see that object without taking the lid off. You decide to cut four holes in the shoebox so you can look inside. You cut one hole in the top, making the top view pane. You cut one hole in the back of the shoebox, making the back view pane. You cut one window on the right of the shoebox, making the right view pane. Now you can see your object from almost any angle as you work on it. These are universally called *orthographic* windows, but it's such a big term that most people just call them *fixed views*. The other view that I didn't mention is the Perspective pane; it shows your object as it would look inside your 3D world, which means you could walk all the way around your object—in other words, you can see the object "in perspective." Get used to working in all four view panes at once because if you just work in one, you might not get the whole picture, and you can really screw up your modeling.

In the Top view pane, place your cursor about three geometric grid squares up from center and three grid squares left from center. The center is where those heavy dark grid lines intersect. Click and drag your cursor down three grid squares right of center and three grid squares down from center, as in Figure 6.4. Then release your mouse button.

You only have a ghost brush for now. It has a frame and red and green anchors on the sides. You can actually grab these anchors and resize the object in any of the fixed views before committing to this brush. Press Enter to commit the brush to your scene. The cube will finally "pop" into existence. The anchor points are gone, but you should see that the cube has a gizmo similar to the Torque World Editor. This gizmo acts in the exact same way and has an arrow handle for X, Y, and Z axes, which you can grab to drag the object around in your scene.

Changing the Crate's Texture

Your crate (for that's what your cube's supposed to be) doesn't look like much of a crate with that horrid orange texture applied to it. This is just one of the default

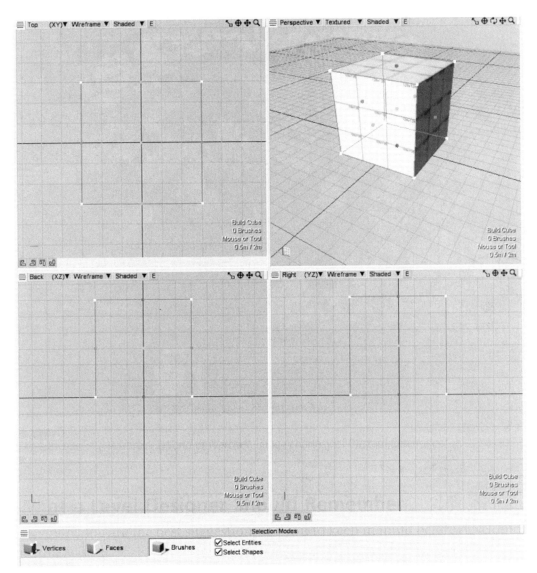

Figure 6.4
Making a basic cube shape in the Top view pane.

textures, which you can see in the Materials form on the right side of your screen (see Figure 6.5). Any time you don't assign a specific texture to an object you create in Constructor, the object will have a texture slapped on it by default, like the orange one with the 128 × 128 written on it here.

There are two good reasons for this. One is that you are constantly reminded by such garish colors that you've forgotten to texture something; and two is that a lot of developers build their whole scene first and use the grid squares on the

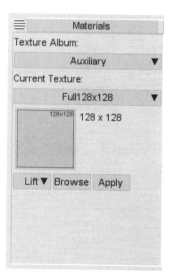

Figure 6.5
The Materials form has a default texture for all new objects.

textures to line up and get proportions right with all their objects before placing realistic textures on them.

Go ahead and click the Browse button just below the default texture's thumbnail. The Texture Browser window will open up. On the left side of this window, there's a tree list of texture albums. There are lots of textures to choose from. Click on Starter to expand its list. Click on the texture s17, and then hit the Make Active button in the lower-right corner of the window. This applies the texture to your selected object. Click on Active & Close to apply the texture, and exit the Texture Browser.

Back in the Constructor window, look in the Perspective view pane to make sure that the crate now has the s17 texture applied to it on all of its faces. That's it; you're through! To save, go to File > Save As and save your work as crate.map in the default Constructor folder.

Tip

You may have to scale textures that appear too big and blurry on an object. To do this, hit the Faces button at the bottom of your screen, and click one of the faces wearing your texture. Look on the left under the Object panel, and you should see Texture: Position, Texture: Justify & Fit, and Texture: Alignment. These three sections have all the tools you need to change the appearance of the texture on the face you have selected. Fitting a texture to an object so that it looks perfect is tedious, but it enhances every level you make in this way.

Exporting the Crate

Now it's time to transform that MAP file into a DIF file that we can actually use in-game. It's easy. Go to File > Export > Torque Game Engine (map2dif plus) and follow the onscreen instructions. Browse to YournameDemo\data\interiors. Click OK. You'll get a window showing you the progress as the MAP file gets converted into a DIF file. When you see the word "Done," you can hit the Close button safely. Don't worry; this isn't a Jekyll-and-Hyde routine. You'll still have a MAP file you can edit in Torque Constructor later, but now you'll also have a DIF file you can actually place into your game.

Importing the Crate into Your Game

Launch YournameDemo and enter the edit mode as you've been doing. Fly up above the terrain, looking down, and aim your cursor at the spot in the game world where you want your crate to go. Open the World Editor Creator, and on the tree list at the lower right, expand the Interiors group by clicking on the plus sign. You should see Crate on the list. Click just once on Crate. Your creation will be spawned where your screen intersects the terrain.

Look around to find your crate. Notice that a little dialog window has popped up, telling you that your scene now needs to be relit. Click the Relight Scene button on the dialog window. You'll see your crate change to its proper textured form, with baked shadows on the terrain and everything, similar to Figure 6.6. If your crate's anything like mine, I made mine too large in comparison to my player character. In the World Editor Inspector, click on the crate and look in its attributes for Transform > Scale, and transform the 1 1 1 into some other numbers, like 0.5 0.5 0.5, which effectively halves the size of the crate.

Tip

Previously, I mentioned that you should relight whenever you change the terrain. Adding DIF objects changes the terrain because it changes the placement of baked-on shadows. So when you add DIF objects, you can click on and move them around a bit, and their textures will appear on them without relighting the scene; but you still need to relight your scene before you forget. You can relight your scenes by choosing Edit > Relight Scene or by pressing ALT+L.

Build a Village

You've created a crate, but now you want to create larger structures, don't you? Ravenscroft is essentially a backwater village, and it needs some homes built for it. Each one should be different. I'll show you how to get started by building one house (see Figure 6.7), and you can construct endless varieties for your game.

Figure 6.6
Your finished crate.

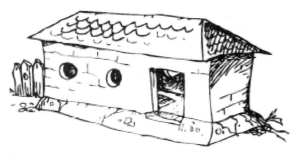

Figure 6.7
A simple Ravenscroft village home.

Making a House

We will make a house in Constructor to put in our game. You might be thinking to yourself, "Isn't a house part of an exterior space?" Yes, it is. But a house is not part of the terrain, and it is also an object that a player might want his character walking inside or on top of. For that to work, the house has to be a DIF. So we're going to make the house with Torque Constructor.

Rev up the Constructor. Pick the cube shape brush (guess what?—this is the most-used brush by most developers). Create a cube brush measuring nine grid spaces in length by six grid spaces in width by eight grid spaces in height. Press Enter to commit the brush to the scene.

Go back and get another cube brush tool and make a second brush inside the first one, nested with about one-half grid unit between them on all sides, as in Figure 6.8. Press Enter, but keep your new rectangle selected (you should see

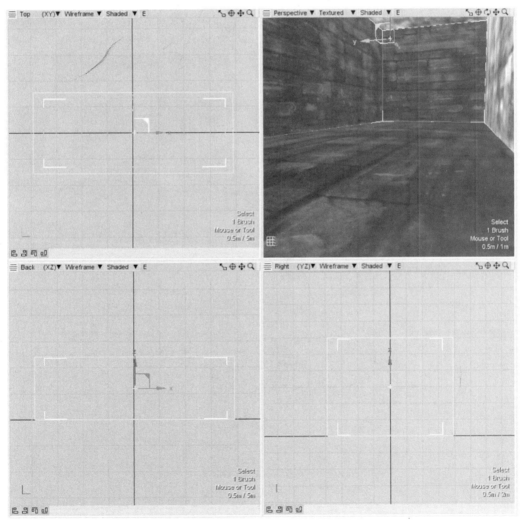

Figure 6.8
Nested cube shapes.

its gizmo). On the side of the Tools form there are several tabs we haven't looked at yet. Click the Modify tab. You'll see a group of icon buttons in the Tools form now. The one on the far left is the CSG Subtract command button. Hit it once.

What you've done is used the second cube shape to subtract its shape from the other, like a giant eraser. You should still have this second cube shape selected. Hit Delete to get rid of it because we don't need it anymore. Your cube is now hollow, but since there aren't any windows or doors, you can't tell that yet in the Perspective view pane.

Back in the Tools form, click the Create tab to bring the brush shapes back. Select the cube again. Make a brush for the door and position it so that its bottom will be fairly flush with the "floor" of the hollow cube, and make sure that it protrudes from the inside to the outside of the hollow cube, as you see can see in Figure 6.9.

Click the Modify tab in the Tools form, and hit the CSG Subtract button once more. This will carve a door in the wall of the hollowed cube. With the door

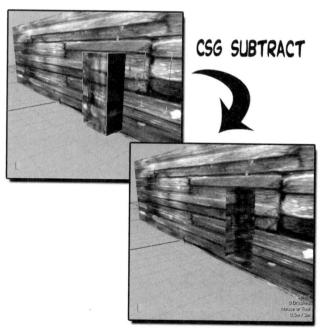

Figure 6.9
Before and after carving a door out of our room.

brush still selected, hit Delete to get rid of it. You should see an empty doorway where there was once a brush shape, as in Figure 6.9.

For the windows, use a cylinder scaled to fit and repeat the same process you used to make the door. This will make round porthole windows in your house. You can reuse the same brush shape for the window instead of deleting it. You can reposition it along another wall and hit Boolean Subtract again to erase another space for a window. Continue to work in this fashion until you have two windows in the back of the house, one in the front, and (optionally) one or more on the sides. Then press Delete to get rid of your versatile cylinder brush.

Go back to the Create Tools form and make another cube brush that matches the width and length of the bottom of the house but extends down another two grid squares. You can use this as a foundation or raised ground plane that you'll sink into your terrain back in the World Editor later.

So far you've only been working in the Brushes selection mode. Now look at the bottom of your screen. You should see buttons for each of the other selection modes available to you, including Brushes, Faces, Edges, and Vertices. You know what Brushes means by now, but you might be kind of unclear as to what the others are for.

- **Faces**—Allows you to control the flat planes or sides of your object.

- **Edges**—Allows you to control the lines or edges on the outside of your object.

- **Vertices**—Allows you to control the corner points (also known as dots, ticks, anchor points, mesh intersection points, and more).

Hit the Vertices button. Anchor points will appear on the corners of your last cube shape. Click and drag your mouse to select the bottom-most row of vertices on this cube. (You should see four dots, or vertices, become highlighted in the Top view pane when you have them all selected.)

In the Tools form, click on the Transform tab and hit the Planar Scale button. Click and drag with the left mouse button to move your four chosen vertices out farther away from each other so that the house's foundation flares out, as in Figure 6.10. To exit out of using the Scale tool, press the Esc key. Go back to Brushes selection mode.

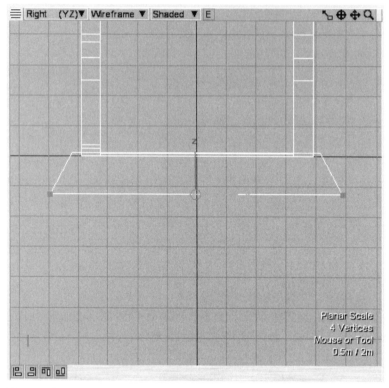

Figure 6.10
Moving vertices to flare out the foundation for the house.

The same method you used to make a foundation under your house you'll use to create a roof.

Create a cube shape that is about the same width and length of the house and about three grid squares high. Move it until it rests on top of the house. Switch to Vertices mode, and select the top row of four vertices on the roof, using the Scale tool to bring them in closer to one another. Then select the bottom row of four vertices on the roof and use the Scale tool to flare them out. This will give the roof a slanted look, like a pitched roof.

You can continue to add niceties, like a chimney stack, a low stone wall extending out past the front or back of the house, a back door, some walls inside, or even furniture. Most of this work would be a repetition of what you've done so far. Otherwise, we're through here.

Texturing a House

I have used one texture for all the walls of the hollow cube making up the majority of the house, another texture for the foundation, and still another texture for the roof. You can apply any textures that you want to your house. If you need to apply separate textures to walls or ceilings, you can enter Face selection mode and pick the faces that you want to adjust individually. You can align, scale, and nudge the textures into place with more precision under the Object tab on the left of the screen. (You might have to do so by entering X, Y, and Z values; it might seem tedious, but it will be worth it.) When you finish, go to File > Save As and save your house as Constructor\house01.map.

Exporting and Using a House

Compile your house using the same method as I showed you for the crate, making a house01.dif in YournameDemo\data\interiors folder. Exit Constructor and launch YournameDemo. Enter the World Editor Creator and find house01 under the expanded Interiors list. Click house01 once to place your DIF into your level. Once you've placed house01 into your level, you can grab it by the gizmo handles and move it anywhere you need it to go. Check Figure 5.8 (the illustration of Ravenscroft) back in Chapter 5 to see the original sketch of where the village lies on our terrain, then relight your level to re-bake shadows. Your house should appear at least as good as Figure 6.11, if not better! Now you have completed one

Figure 6.11
Your finished home.

house, but a village rarely consists of just one house. So either place a few more house01 DIFs into your level, arranging them into various poses and scaling them so they look slightly different from each other, or go back into the Torque Constructor and make more. You can add endless variety to your homes. The more practice you get building in the CSG editor, the better your homes will start to look, until you glance back at your first one, house01, and say, "Man, did I make that? That's just downright ugly!" By the way, I had you call your first home house01. The next ones you make should continue that naming convention: house02, house03, house04, and house05.

Build a Church

At the hub of your game level, the tallest building in Ravenscroft, standing silhouetted on a hilltop and dead-center of the ancestral graveyard, rests the gray-shouldered church. You've built a teensy crate. You've wrestled with a walk-in domicile. Now it's time to pack everything you've learned into constructing this church.

If you still feel uncomfortable with Constructor, or if you don't trust your own artistic skills here, you can look at the church layout in Figure 6.12 and make most of the blocks literally just blocks, or cube shapes, in those approximate positions and then texture them. However, if you are starting to get your creative juices flowing, and you are getting the LEGO or Lincoln Logs engineering feeling in your bones, experiment as much as you like. Use some other brushes. Switch between the different selection and transform modes, and play with them all. Put together your best artwork in the church. Remember, this construction is not only meant to serve as a landmark, it is also a playground that the player will be able to go inside and move around in.

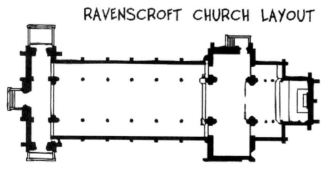

Figure 6.12
The church layout.

From this point on, your imagination will be the only limit. You can build castles, sewer tunnels, underground complexes, military bases, city streets, factories, and just about any other man-made structure with the Torque Constructor.

Review

In this chapter you should have learned the following:

- What the differences are between DTS and DIF files.

- What CSG (Constructive Solid Geometry) modeling is all about.

- What the most prominent features are of the Torque Constructor.

- How to use brushes to make objects, both small and large, in your scene.

- How to move, transform, and texture these objects.

- How to use brushes to subtract from other shapes using the Boolean Subtract tool.

- How to switch between selection modes and what those selection modes are.

- How to save your scene and export it as a DIF.

- How to import DIFs into your game level using the World Editor Creator.

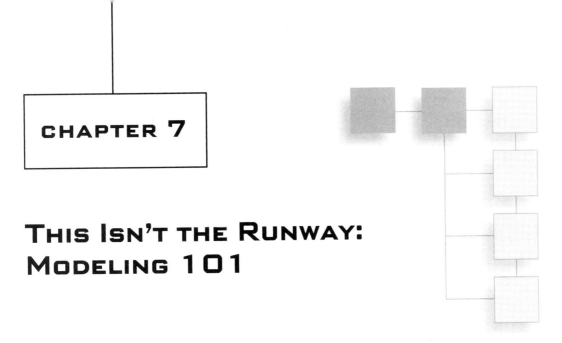

CHAPTER 7

THIS ISN'T THE RUNWAY: MODELING 101

What you look at over half the time that you're playing video games (and what most players base their purchase of a new game on to start with) is the artwork. Artwork that got started with 8-bit graphics has utterly exploded in the gaming industry, and today it stands as a very important part of game design. Your artwork will either attract users to your games or put them off before they even play them. Part of your artwork is 2D, and it gets used for the interface. The rest is 3D, and I'm not talking about the terrain.

3D Does Not Require Special Glasses!

It's vital to know how to make 3D models, how to get your models into Torque, and also how to model efficiently for a real-time game engine.

This last part takes some explaining. Unlike 3D films like *Shrek the Third* (see Figure 7.1), a game engine must be able to render huge amounts of geometry and effects in real time. In order to do this, the game engine relies heavily on the user's computer and how much virtual memory it has. Shortcuts are taken in the rendering process to optimize frame rate on any computer screen. Torque has its own unique shortcuts. One shortcut is to make low-poly models; another is the use of DTS files for models. We'll discuss the finer points of DTS later. Right now, let's take a closer look at low-poly modeling.

Figure 7.1
Shrek the Third (image courtesy of DreamWorks Animation LLC, 2007).

Low-Poly Modeling

In order to understand what is meant by "low-poly," you must first have a firm grasp of 3D space. Perhaps you are already something of a 3D artist, or perhaps the tutorials so far in this book have taught you a great deal about working in 3D. If you already think you know all about 3D, skip over the next section. If not, read on.

A Short Lesson in 3D

Those geometry lessons in school should really come in handy because, when you learn geometry, you're learning the concepts behind virtual space, or 3D. 3D space has height, width, and depth, which are often measured by the Cartesian coordinates X, Y, and Z. The following is terminology most often referred to when working in 3D:

- A point in 3D space is called a *vertex* (or point, dot, or tick, depending on which program you're using).

- Lines that run between vertices are *edges*.

- There are two types of faces: triangles and polygons.

- The plane made up by three intersecting edges is a *triangle*.

- *Polygons* are often witnessed as squares made up of two (or more) triangles.

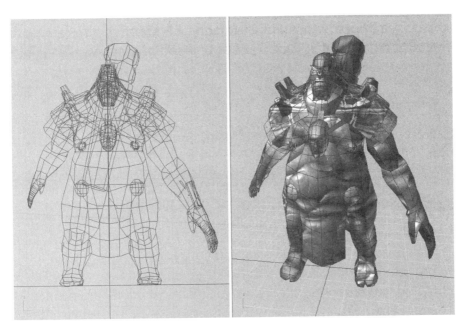

Figure 7.2
A texture applied to the surface of a mesh in Max.

- Polygons interconnect to form a wireframe outline of a model; this wireframe is called a *mesh.*

- A *surface* is the outside of the mesh, which you put a texture or material on (see Figure 7.2).

This is a lot of information to digest right away, so re-read this last bit if you're still lost; and if you still don't get it, just continue right along because it will eventually come to you through practice with 3D software.

From Sprite to 3D

In the first generation of electronic gaming, back in the golden years of Atari and the first Nintendo, graphics were not 3D but only 8-bit sprite images. Pixels at that time were large colored squares, and characters couldn't have a whole lot of details. In the second generation, when we had the first burgeoning of Super Nintendo, Nintendo 64, SEGA Genesis, and Playstation, games truly entered the 3D spectrum, but they were still limited to around 600 polygons per character. Pixels had shrunk but were still very noticeable. Now in the "next gen," or third generation, of games, with higher-rate computer processors and better video cards, characters are limited to around 1,000 polys, and pixels are so minute that displays look flawlessly detailed even when you stare at them a while.

Tricks to Defeat Rendering Lag

Cinema that uses CG (computer graphics) is composed of several layers of 3D renderings over time. You don't have this luxury in a game. Games are meant to be played in real time, and the rendering can only be as good as the user's video hardware, as previously mentioned. Thus game asset artists have tried many tricks to keep the rendering time low and the game moving at a rapid pace.

One trick has always been to limit the visibility of any one screenshot. For instance, if you are going to show the player an entire alien landscape, with sharp protruding mountains on the horizon and villages in the valley, without taking any shortcuts, you will cause the player to have difficulty with the frame rate. This is why most games take place in twisting corridors and with limited visibility. Or they use another trick, which I'm going to tell you about in just a moment.

Another trick is to limit the number of polygons in any given scene. As previously mentioned, a good rule of thumb with today's games is keeping polys for each character under 1,000. Overall, using fewer polygons on a character can make it look less smooth and less realistic, but making better texture maps to cover the model can hide this fact. Painting in just the right amount of light, shadow, and detail in the 2D texture map can make a relatively flat character come to life.

The other trick I promised to mention is using level of detail, or LOD. LOD is a programming algorithm whereby characters that appear closer to the screen have more polygons, and characters farther away are swapped for models with fewer polygons, until they are nearly blurred beyond all recognition. I will show you how to do this in Torque because it's easy.

All these tricks (limiting visibility, using lower polygon counts, painting better texture maps, and incorporating LOD) save processing time and decrease lag.

Making Game Characters

Tip

"Be your character what it will, it will be known; and nobody will take it upon your word."

—Philip Dormer Shanhope, Lord Chesterfield

Figure 7.3
A lineup of villains from *City of Villains* (image courtesy of NCsoft, 2007).

Character creation, especially if you've never played a role-playing game yourself, can seem complicated at first. Let me clue you in on the quickest and easiest ways to come up with fresh original characters.

Is there such a thing as an original character? Psychologist Carl Jung says not, that most people categorize others into neat classifications, which he called *archetypes*. So of hero archetypes, there might be the White Knight, the Moody Rogue, the Tough Brute, the Scholarly Wizard, and much more (for a lineup of villains, see Figure 7.3). The difficult article about archetypes is drawing the line between a true archetype and a clichéd stereotype. Don't use clichés, because most players are sick of them.

Types of Game Characters

With possibly the exception of puzzle games and the ever-popular Tetris, most games have characters in them. Even vehicles and weapons, in their own unique way, are characters in a game. There are, however, three major types of game characters that we see over and over again:

- **Player Characters**—The player's onscreen avatar, or the character the player has direct control over, which has to look good because it takes up

Figure 7.4
One example of a disinterested party (I mean, NPC).

nearly 90% of screen time and may indeed become an icon for the game itself.

- **Non-player Characters**—Also known as NPCs, these are any of the other characters that the player cannot directly control that may help, hinder, or advise the player during the course of the game (like the lady in Figure 7.4).

- **Enemies**—Technically these bad guys are non-player characters, but since they perform a very specific role (and depending on the genre, they may even have a central role in the game, like targets in a first person shooter), enemies are those characters that try to defeat the player.

Artificially Intelligent

AI stands for the TV program *American Idol,* but it also stands for artificial intelligence, a complex programming that makes non-player characters appear to have sentience or the ability to think for themselves. In other words, AI is where the computer controls a character. The way the game software controls characters is through several subroutines.

Game characters are becoming more and more lifelike because programmers are getting better and better at developing AI. NPCs don't just stand there looking pretty or run around shooting anymore; they can have complex emotional simulations and react to players with human characteristics. Gamers expect more beautiful graphics, and because gamers are the ones who pay the overhead, game developers are focusing on more sophisticated characters.

Character Descriptions

For your game design document, you need to describe all the characters that show up in the game. Descriptions should include illustrations, model sheets, and text descriptions.

Writing Text Descriptions

You should begin with text descriptions. Depending on the importance of each character and the scope of the game project, these descriptions can be one paragraph or one page long. What the development team needs to know is enough information to flesh out a dull character, like the following questions:

- What type of character is it?

- What archetype best fits your character?

- What role or occupation does your character fulfill?

- What is your character's overall personality?

- What does your character look like? What is its race, size, gender, and general look?

- What does your character wear? Does its outfit match its occupation and personality?

If you have trouble envisioning your character, imagine sitting down at lunch with your character (or something else totally mundane) and asking him questions about himself. You may also look at the characters in books, comic books, and movies that you like. Just fill in the blanks, and you'll be surprised how interesting your characters will become.

Sketching Your Description

Once you have a rough idea in words about your character, it'll become easier for you to sketch the character on paper (that is, given you are an artist of any caliber). Draw concept artwork of what the character will look like. Think in 3D, even while you're drawing in 2D. In fact, most concept artwork of characters comes in the form of model sheets, which look like police lineups and mug shots in a way; the character is viewed from the front, side, side, and back, and then is asked to make a bunch of faces at the camera! Model sheets may look funny, but

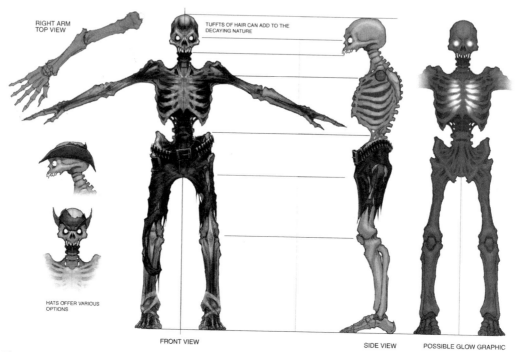

RIGHT ARM
TOP VIEW

TUFFTS OF HAIR CAN ADD TO THE
DECAYING NATURE

HATS OFFER VARIOUS
OPTIONS

FRONT VIEW

SIDE VIEW

POSSIBLE GLOW GRAPHIC

Figure 7.5
Model sheet from the game *Darkwatch* (image courtesy of High Moon Studios, 2007).

they let the team that makes the models for the characters know what this character looks like from any angle and in any pose. Some, like Figure 7.5, show variations of one type of stock character.

I No Ditz, I Know DTS

DTS is a 3D model format optimized for rendering in Torque. The following list outlines the kinds of models the DTS format is designed for:

- Character models animated using bones.

- Small complex objects such as rocks, trees, chairs, tables, weapons, ammo packs, flags and more, which can also be animated or attached to player or vehicle models.

- Vehicles, which player character models and weapons can be mounted onto.

- Dynamic animated details to be added to DIF structures, such as turret cannons, revolving radio dishes, roosting birds, and more.

We looked at the major distinction between DIF and DTS files in the last chapter, but essentially, a DIF file is good for man-made structures, like the crates, houses, and church you made, as well as any object that players will have to walk on top of or inside of. A DTS file is good for animated characters, vehicles, weapons, items, and more.

In this chapter, we'll look at the creation of DTS files using several of the most widely used modeling packages in the industry, and we'll also create the player character for our *Abandon All Hope* game: Little Reaper!

Most Widely Used Modeling Packages for Creating DTS Files

It can be tricky figuring out which modeling package to use for Torque, as there isn't currently a modeling program made specifically for Torque.

The top two industry-standard packages model artists use in game design are 3ds Max (or just plain Max) and Maya—both of which can be purchased from Autodesk. Max and Maya help you create super-efficient 3D models and, using special plug-in exporters, can export them to DTS files. However, both programs can cost you quite a bit of money, so be prepared for it.

On the other hand, there are low-budget options. The most commonly sought program for Torque developers on a shoestring is MilkShape 3D, which has similar tools to Max or Maya but is quite a bit cheaper. Chumbalum Soft makes MilkShape 3D, and you can download their program from chumbalum. swissquake.ch on the Web. MilkShape 3D also has a plug-in exporter you can use to export files to DTS.

Another modeling program, Blender, is open-source (which means free!). You will find the installer files for Blender on the companion CD-ROM in the software folder. There's a different Blender installer for each operating system. For the Windows build of Blender, you may need to install an official update from Microsoft called Microsoft Visual C++ 2005 Redistributable Package (x86). Vista doesn't need this, but users of older Windows versions should install it if they experience a crash during the startup of Blender. You can look it up online at Microsoft's Web site. If you do decide to use Blender, the Torque DTS exporter for Windows is also on the companion CD-ROM in its own folder under software. A really good reference book is *The Official Blender 2.3 Guide: Free 3D Creation Suite for Modeling, Animation, and Rendering* by Ton Roosendaal and Stefano Selleri (No Starch Press, 2005).

Using 3ds Max for Making DTS Files

I will be using 3ds Max 9 for the following modeling tutorials, but the same basic principles apply no matter what program you get your mitts on, so I believe you can still follow along. If you would like to use 3ds Max 9, you can download a 30-day trial version of it from Autodesk. Just Google for "3ds max trial," and you'll find the latest-and-greatest software trial online. And no, before you start asking, the free alternative program Gmax does not work for Torque, so you can't use it.

The Torque DTS Exporter is a plug-in for 3ds Max. There is one that works for 3ds Max 4 through 5, another for 3ds Max 6, 7, and 8, and another for 3ds Max 9. They are all named Max2dtsExporter.dle. It's up to you to look them up online (you might use Google to browse the Web for the correct download), download them, and keep them straight. Place the appropriate file for your version of 3ds Max into the plug-ins folder of 3ds Max. Then restart 3ds Max in order for the plug-in to be seen by the software.

A really good resource for using 3ds Max to create DTS files for Torque is Brad Strong's book *Creating Game Art for 3D Engines* (Thomson Course Technology, 2007). He covers additional tips and tricks for using Max to create assets for Torque, so if you find this to be an area you enjoy, be sure to pick up his book.

Modeling Little Reaper

Take a look at Little Reaper, as I've sketched him in Figure 7.6. This is the model sheet we'll be using.

Figure 7.6
The Little Reaper character model sheet.

There are several options for creating characters for Torque. Since we'll be exporting Little Reaper to replace the player character in the FPS Starter Kit (our old buddy Korkis), all we really have to do is replace the DTS file and the config file and make sure our animations export correctly.

3D artists use a wide variety of techniques to make low-poly game models. They start with a blank slate and, using a twist and whirl of the cursor, create life-like characters. Okay, so it's not that easy. . . . In fact, it's downright time-consuming, and you must have a lot of patience to do it at all. Never mind that for now. Model artists have developed several techniques that have become standard today, and we'll be using the most popular one: box and segmented modeling.

Box and Segmented Modeling

One of the most popular methods for low-poly construction is box modeling. Box modeling starts with a primitive shape (most often a box or cylinder) that gets subdivided into multiple smaller faces that are moved and transformed into the shape required. Box modeling is also good because it gives us a clear seam when it comes to unwrapping the model to texture it.

Many artists for film and print make smooth whole characters, but for low-poly characters in games, artists typically make them out of multiple segments and stick them together like construction sets. Artists may make a leg here, an arm there, then a torso and head; when they are all through, they wedge them together, either using a skeleton rig underneath or through the engine's programming.

Remember to Build Only Structurally Sound Models

Before we begin, I want to remind you that it is imperative to build only structurally sound models. Leaving mistakes in a model or making a poorly constructed model and then hoping that it will still work is never enough. The main problems to look out for as you build are

- **Stray Vertices**—Those vertices that do not tie at least three edges together or float out in space without anything to connect them.

- **T junctions**—Edges that do not meet with other edges correctly, either overlapping or stopping short of meeting other edges.

- **Sliver Planes**—Those triangles or polygons that are so thin that their corners where edges meet are often less than 35 degrees or greater than 190 degrees.

Editable Poly versus Editable Mesh

For Torque, your model must be composed of triangles instead of polygons. Therefore, when working with 3ds Max, you must convert your model to Editable Mesh (which is made up of triangles) before you export. Your face count is also dependent on triangles, not polys (as a triangle is equally the same as a face), and Torque suggests a maximum of 500 faces for weapons and smaller objects and a maximum of 2,250 faces for detailed characters. The Korkis orc model, for instance, has a total of 1,900 faces. This is a short budget to work with, but it is absolutely doable. In 3ds Max, you can count faces by pressing the 7 key or by using the Polygon Counter (found under Utilities > More > Polygon Counter). You can also count faces by this simple arithmetic: 1 polygon = 2 triangles or faces.

Units of Measurement

Torque requires some precise size measurements when working in external software programs like 3ds Max. For instance, Torque is based on the metric system. So the first thing that you must do before starting a new shape in 3ds Max is to select Customize > Units Setup > Select Metric and make sure that 1 unit is set to 1 meter. This gives you the correct scale in 3ds Max for exporting to Torque, where a standard human is 2 meters tall.

Working Off a Template

Most artists do not work in a void. Model artists usually take the model sheets that sketch artists put together and build templates to model from. Typically a front and side shot are enough to form templates to build the character around. It's usually recommended to model characters from a pose such as Leonardo's Vitruvian Man (see Figure 7.7).

You can find the templates Reaper_Front.jpg and Reaper_Side.jpg on the companion CD-ROM under projects/Chapter 7.

Take a brief moment to familiarize yourself with Max, if you haven't already. In Max 9, there are Essential Skills movies that are playable at startup. Review the movies for User Interface Overview, Viewport Navigation, Creating Objects, Transforming Objects, Modifying Objects, and Materials in order to get your feet wet and prepare for the next stage. If you have any troubles, you can also visit Help > Tutorials for a wide range of well-crafted tutorials on how to create and modify models in Max.

Figure 7.7
The Vitruvian Man by Leonardo DaVinci.

You should study Figure 7.8 to guide you as you follow along with this project. You can minimize or maximize selected viewports by pressing Alt+W, and while in one viewport you can swap to the next one by pressing F for front view, P for perspective, U for user, L for left, and R for right. This will help because often times it's necessary to zoom in on a single view when adding detail work.

Right-click on the left viewport's title bar and change the left viewport to a right side view. Then create two planes, one that is flat to this right side view and one that is flat to the front view. In Max, creating primitive shapes is done either through the Create panel toolbox on the right or by going to the menu bar under Create. Click in one of the viewports and drag your mouse to create the size of the plane you want. Both of your planes should be centered on origin (0 0 0) in Max, thus they should intersect perfectly. Use the grid to orient (hotkey G) and turn on the 3D Snap tool in conjunction with using the Move tool to make sure that objects being manipulated snap directly to the grid. Check the perspective or user viewport to make sure that they're placed exactly.

With both planes oriented, snapped, and placed in the correct positions, you can add the template images to them. Be sure to place the Reaper_Front.jpg over the front view plane and the Reaper_Side.jpg over the right view plane. To place

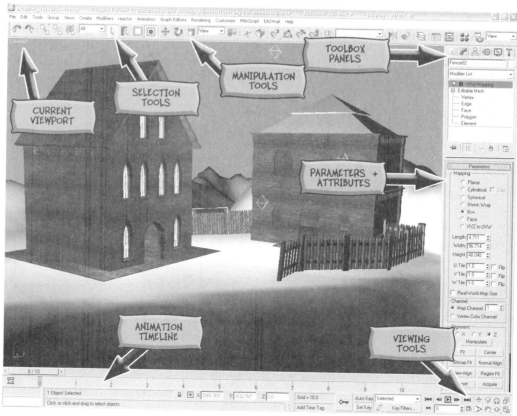

Figure 7.8
The Max interface.

these images, click on each plane and add a UVW Map modifier to them with
Bitmap Fit selected. Press the M key to open the Material Editor. This is the
interface you use to place textures on shapes. With the projects\Chapter 7 folder
open, click-drag Reaper_Front.jpg to the first default texture sphere in the
Material Editor and let go. Reaper_Front.jpg will now appear, wrapping the first
default texture sphere. Click in the name field where it says default 01 and call this
material fronttemp. Repeat with Reaper_Side.jpg, calling it backtemp.

With the front view plane selected, click on the fronttemp material and press the
Apply to Object button (found in Figure 7.9). You might have to check the Show
Map in Viewport box to get the templates to show up in Max. After you see the
materials appear on the planes, you may need to adjust them slightly so that the
top of the head, the chin, and the body line up. Next you have to freeze the planes.
Right-click each plane, go to Properties, and check the box next to Freeze. Make
sure to uncheck Show Frozen in Gray (otherwise your frozen objects turn gray,
and you'll not be able to see the actual template), then click OK.

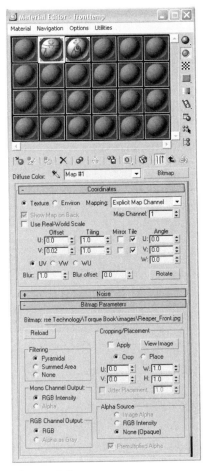

Figure 7.9
The Material Editor in Max.

You should now have a workable template. This allows you to keep your scale and shapes consistent as you build Little Reaper.

Modeling the Head

Create a primitive shape, like a geosphere, which can be found under Extended Primitives. You could also start with a cylinder or with a box; it's up to you, whatever is easiest for you to manipulate. I use a geosphere rather than a basic sphere because geospheres are easier to unwrap and texture later. When creating a shape more complex than a plane, you have to click-drag to create one depth of dimension and, when you release the mouse, you move it again to create the second depth of dimension. Click again to close the shape.

With the Move tool, drag the geosphere up to the place on the templates where the head should go. Notice that using the Move, Scale, or Rotate tools inspires the gizmo that you should recognize from the Torque Editor: it has three handles, one for each Cartesian coordinate (X, Y, and Z), and they're colored the same.

Make the geosphere semi-transparent by right-clicking on it, go into Properties, check See-Through, and click OK. Right-click on it again and select Convert to > Convert to Editable Poly. Notice that your toolbox on the right has switched to Modify, and you now have a list tree of sub-object modes you can enter at will to modify the separate parts of the shape, including Vertex, Edge, Face, and Element (see Figure 7.10).

Figure 7.10
The sub-object modes under the Modify tab.

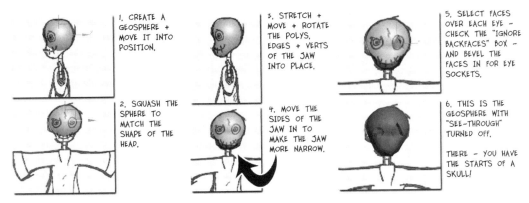

Figure 7.11
Construction of Little Reaper's skull.

When you click on one of these sub-object modes, you can only adjust that sub-object type. The sub-object in the list tree will turn yellow. Click on it again, and you'll leave the sub-object mode and return to manipulating the original object. You're essentially locked in when working in sub-object modes. This means that you cannot add modifiers to the whole object or change other parts of the object or any other object until you leave sub-object mode.

Try adjusting the vertices, polys, and edges of your geosphere until it correctly matches the shape of the head in the templates. As you can tell from the templates, we're going to go all Rayman style with this character, so his head does not have to connect to his body and his body does not have to connect to his hands or feet. This gives you a lot of leeway. You can follow the steps as I've outlined them in Figure 7.11. If you have any troubles reading the information from the illustrations in this book, you can see them at their original size on the companion CD in the figures folder.

Modeling the Torso

The torso can start with a cylinder, but it must be stretched out so that it's taller than the skull. Remember to make this cylinder semi-transparent and convert it to an Editable Poly in the same way we did the head. Use the various sub-object modes and your own aesthetic choices to shape the torso so that it fits the body shape of the templates.

Go ahead and stretch the bottom out to form the bottom of Reaper's gown. To make arms, first select the polys on the side of his torso, turn on the Slice Plane button, and then click on the Slice button. This cuts the selected polys so you have smaller polys to select from. Select one of the smaller faces on his side,

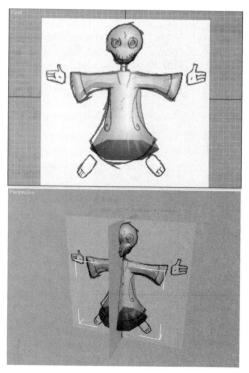

Figure 7.12
Little Reaper's torso.

Extrude or Bevel it (using the Modify toolbox's Extrude or Bevel buttons), make an adjustment by rotating or scaling the selected end of the arm, and repeat. As you go through this cycle, attempt to match the template with your model. You will want to work in the front view primarily, but every so often check your perspective view and right side view to make sure you're not deviating. When you're through you should have an image similar to Figure 7.12.

Modeling the Hands and Feet

Little Reaper's feet and hands should be modeled from four separate box primitives, with one end of them beveled out to form the toes and fingers. We could model each finger or toe individually, but as this is a first-person shooter game that we're making, such detail would be lost to the player. Plus, it helps us keep the face count down if we limit ourselves. Follow the steps in Figure 7.13 to make a hand, and then repeat the process for the other hand and the feet (with the exception that feet don't need thumbs!).

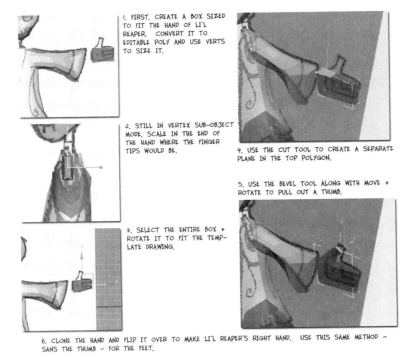

1. FIRST, CREATE A BOX SIZED TO FIT THE HAND OF LI'L REAPER. CONVERT IT TO EDITABLE POLY AND USE VERTS TO SIZE IT.

2. STILL IN VERTEX SUB-OBJECT MODE, SCALE IN THE END OF THE HAND WHERE THE FINGER TIPS WOULD BE.

3. SELECT THE ENTIRE BOX + ROTATE IT TO FIT THE TEMP-LATE DRAWING.

4. USE THE CUT TOOL TO CREATE A SEPARATE PLANE IN THE TOP POLYGON.

5. USE THE BEVEL TOOL ALONG WITH MOVE + ROTATE TO PULL OUT A THUMB.

6. CLONE THE HAND AND FLIP IT OVER TO MAKE LI'L REAPER'S RIGHT HAND.   USE THIS SAME METHOD – SANS THE THUMB – FOR THE FEET.

Figure 7.13
Constructing Little Reaper's hand.

Unwrapping and Skinning Little Reaper

Before rigging the model or doing anything else with it, you must put a texture on it. Before adding a texture to the mesh, check every inch of it for stray vertices, T junctions, and sliver planes and, if you find any, fix them first. Then select the template planes and press Delete to get rid of them because you won't need them again.

Now select each of the following shapes one by one: the body, the hands, and the feet. From the Modifiers list, add a UVW Map modifier to each one. The textures we want to use are in the projects\Chapter 7 folder on the companion CD-ROM. The body should get the cloak.jpg texture, while the hands and feet should get the bony.jpg texture. You can play around with the UV mapping in the Modify toolbox. Try Shrinkwrap, Box, or Cylindrical mapping for the body. Either Box or Shrinkwrap will be the best mapping choices for the hands and feet.

For Little Reaper's skull you want to use a different modifier: Unwrap UVW. Once you've added the Unwrap UVW modifier, see how the texture lies on the model. For a default texture, I usually use a Checker one, which is a black-and-white checkerboard pattern. If you want to use this too, select a new sample texture slot, click the button to the right of Diffuse in the Blinn Basic Parameters rollout, and select the Checker material from the available list. You can adjust the size and number of checkers with Tiling under the Coordinates rollout.

Once you're satisfied that the mapping looks fairly decent, click the Edit button to open the Edit UVWs dialog box. Here you can arrange the UVWs so that they'll be easier to paint over. You are essentially unwrapping the 3D shape and flattening it out so that you can paint every part of it effortlessly. The default settings for the Edit UVWs dialog box can make things harder on you. Turn off the background map and grid and uncheck the Constant Update in Viewports checkbox. You have a lot of the same tools in the Edit UVWs dialog box as you do in the regular Max interface, including the ability to move, scale, and rotate, but the manipulations only affect the UVWs. It'll take some time to get used to this interface, but once you do, you'll realize how great it is.

When you're done, you can export the material for editing in Photoshop. Go to Tools > Render UVW to Template to open the Render UVs dialog box. After you've invoked the Render Output tool, set the width and height values for the image to 256 × 256. Click the Render UVW Template button at the bottom of the Render UVs dialog box to bring up the Render Map dialog box. Click the Save Bitmap button on the left side of the dialog box. It is recommended that you use TIF or TGA because JPGs have a vaguely fuzzy look. Now you can use Photoshop or another paint program (like Paint Dot Net) to paint a texture over the UV template, which you can re-import to Max and use as a material on the skull. Figure 7.14 shows you one example of how this can be done.

Rigging Little Reaper

A skeleton rig is not a real skeleton, by any means. It is a simple framework of bones that have the model skinned over the top of them. The bones share interlinked chains that allow for easier animation. Most artists use IK, or *inverse kinematics*, for handling the rig. IK sounds like a complicated phrase, but really it's just a rag-doll control. With IK handlers, you can move a character's hand and his arm will bend and follow, or you twist his foot out to the side and his leg will turn and his knee will bend. These rigs make animating each pose a snap. So if you hear someone mention inverse kinematics, don't cringe—just think, "Hey, that's cool!"

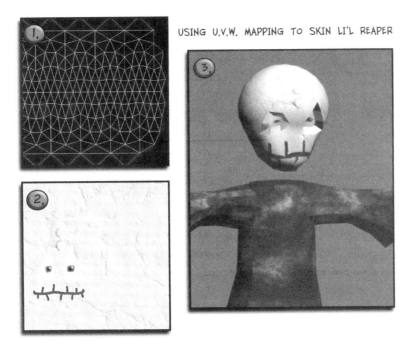

USING U.V.W. MAPPING TO SKIN LI'L REAPER

Figure 7.14
Little Reaper gets a head.

There are two ways to create a skeleton for your character mesh: bones and biped. The biped skeleton is a pre-canned skeleton rig you can use for bipedal characters (such as our friend Korkis or Little Reaper here). With a little ingenuity and some tweaking, you can make a biped customized to fit your character without having to create a bones rig from scratch.

We're going to use the default player biped from the Korkis player model file that comes with the Torque Game Engine in combination with our custom Little Reaper mesh so that we can take advantage of the pre-existing animations. Using the default biped allows us to have all the animating done for us, plus we don't have to spend any time scripting special TorqueScript animations. This saves us a lot of time and effort. On the other hand, using the default biped means we cannot edit the pre-existing animations or add new bones to the skeleton. In other words, the character's animations will look a little canned and mal-formations of the mesh may occur.

If you feel like you want to create and program your own original animations, then you should really pick up a copy of Brad Strong's book *Creating Game Art for 3D Engines,* mentioned previously. I'll show you how to use the provided biped.

Make a copy of the player.max file (in the data\shapes\player folder of your game) and open it. Using Select by Name, find Multires::bodymesh and body-mesh and delete them both. Import your mesh and name it bodymesh3. This is meant to correspond with the detail marker Detail3. Make sure Detail3 is a child of Bip01 (which is the model's Center of Mass, or COM). Delete any other detail markers, and then if necessary adjust your mesh to match the biped's position in the first frame of animation in the idle pose. Once you've done all that, add the Skin modifier to your mesh.

With the Skin modifier on, your Modify toolbox will alter. At the bottom is a listing of bones applied to the mesh skinning; so far there are none. Click Add Bones to add the bones of the player biped. Some of the bones will not get vertex weights attached, but if they don't get any, the model won't export correctly. Spend some time adjusting the vertex weights and how your mesh corresponds with the biped.

You should now have a workable character file to replace the Korkis one. The next sections point out some important information about how characters are handled in Torque, but if you want to at this point you can skip down to the section, "Exporting Little Reaper to DTS."

Embedding Animations

Every move a game character makes—whether it's jumping high in the air, unleashing a combo of attack moves on an opponent, or just plain sallying about—is determined by an animated pose, which is usually a loop of framed animation about 10 to 30 frames long.

Most 3D programs support frame animation, which means that there's an obvious timeline at the top or bottom of the interface that allows you to scroll through frame after frame. You can set poses for keyframes and save them. The program will fill in the gaps with smooth interpolation. Most programs also allow you to name animated sequences separate from one another. You can see the animated sequences in playback, and depending on your settings, most often you'll see the animation run at 24 frames per second (your TV set runs at 30 frames per second).

Most game engines, including Torque, have algorithms that look for animation sequences to render the character models appropriate to the player's actions. So when a character is running, the game engine searches through his animations for a "run animation," and that's the part of animation that it plays.

Torque has built-in support for embedded animations. Torque takes the DTS file and looks for DSQ files that correspond to the naming convention listed below. The naming convention is fairly self-explanatory, as long as you stick with it. Of course, when you get more advanced you can invent your own animations and script handlers for them. The default player biped has many of these already built-in.

- **root**—Character is standing around, breathing, fidgeting, and idle.

- **walk**—Character is walking forward.

- **run**—Character is running forward.

- **jump**—Character is jumping while running.

- **standjump**—Character is jumping from a standing position.

- **fall**—Character is falling off a vertical climb, such as a cliff or tall building.

- **land**—Character lands safely on his feet and gets back up.

- **back**—Character is stepping backward at a fast pace.

- **side**—Character is running sideways or "strafing."

- **sitting**—Character is sitting in a chair or riding in a vehicle.

- **scoutroot**—Character is riding a horse or motorbike.

- **death1 to death11**—Character dies. You don't have to make all 11, but the engine will randomly select one of them to play each time the character dies. Having more for the engine to choose from adds variety.

- **look**—Character points to where he's looking.

- **celwave**—This plays when the player presses CTRL+W (Win) or CMD+W (Mac). It's meant for the character to wave to other characters in online play.

- **celsalute**—This plays when the player presses CTRL+S (Win) or CMD+S (Mac). It's meant for the character to salute or taunt other characters in online play.

Note

If you are just creating a single animated object, such as a flag waving in the wind or a rotating cube, you build the mesh, texture it, skip the whole part about the skeleton, and then you animate the object for a single animation cycle. You also have to set it up so that its animation will loop. To do that, you make sure that the frame position it ends on is the exact same as the frame position it starts on (you can copy and paste keyframes in Max to make this happen). You name your mesh with a 2 on the end, such as Health2 or Weapon2. Then you set up three dummy objects in Max, one called start01, one called base01, and one called Detail2 (all at 0 0 0), with start01 and Detail2 as the child of base01, and start01 as the parent of the mesh. Last, you have to set up Sequence objects (Creat > Helpers > General DTS Objects), right-click on a viewport to enter the Curve Editor, and locate the Sequence object's Start and End tracks. This is so that when you export the file, Torque knows that the object is animated, as well as which frame to start on and which frame to end on.

Embedding Dummy Objects or Markers

The default player biped already has these markers, but if you're creating a new character from scratch you must employ the following:

- **Start01**—One of three must-have objects that is the parent of the main model mesh.

- **Base01**—One of three must-have objects that is the parent of start01 and Detail2.

- **Detail2**—One of three must-have objects that refer to the main mesh, as long as that mesh ends with the number 2.

- **Bounds**—The bounds box, which encloses the character up until his death animations; the bounds box is used for collision detection in the Torque Game Engine.

- **Cam**—The third-person camera object, or where the camera will be positioned when the player switches to third-person mode. This is often behind the player's head.

- **Eye**—The first-person camera object, or where the player's viewpoint will be when starting in first-person. This is often in front of the player's head.

- **Mount0**—Typically positioned near the right hand of the player model, this marker tells the game where to spawn the player's weapon; a weapon model, just so you know, would have a corresponding mountpoint marker.

Dummy objects can be simple box shapes, but they are hidden. The most important things about dummy objects are their names and positions.

Exporting Little Reaper to DTS

Before you go through the export process, there are some important details that your work must conform to every time:

- The character mesh must have triangles (be converted to an Editable Mesh).

- The character is facing the back view.

- The character is standing at 0 0 0.

- There is a detail marker/dummy object called start01 at 0 0 0.

- There is a detail marker/dummy object called base01 at 0 0 0.

- There is a detail marker/dummy object called Detail2 at 0 0 0.

- The base01 marker is the parent of start01 and Detail2.

- The start01 marker is the parent of the main model mesh, and that mesh ends with a 2.

- A simple box shape (often hidden), called bounds, envelops the character for collision detection purposes.

- The Skin modifier uses only those bones used in the animations (about 19 of 29).

- Every vertex in the mesh has been assigned a bone.

- All bones have at least one vertex assigned to them.

- Bones are not named with numbers at the end, so they're not confused for detail objects.

- One config file resides in the folder you are exporting to.

- The MAX file resides in the folder you are exporting to.

If you've followed the project tutorial above and used the default player biped, you shouldn't have much of a problem. Remember to check the direction the character is facing. If the model's not an Editable Mesh already, right-click and select Convert To > Convert To Editable Mesh right before you export, and I'll show you how to write a config file.

Make sure you have just one config file in the folder you're exporting to (in this case, the data\shapes\folder). Your config file should look similar to the default player.cfg file already in that folder. This file has headings for AlwaysExport, NeverExport, and Delete. This config file should be used as is unless you have different export needs or if there are other bones you want to include or exclude.

Once the markers are in place, the hierarchy is complete, and all the key files are present in the player folder (the MAX file, the config file, and any texture files), it is time to export the DTS shape for the character. After you've installed the Torque DTS Exporter that is appropriate for your version of Max, you'll find the Exporter itself under the Utilities tab in the right toolbox panel. When launching the Exporter from within Max, use the typical setup for the most part.

Error Control should have Allow Empty Subtrees, Allow Unused Meshes, and Allow Old Style Sequences checked. Dump File Control should have all options checked in order to generate the most complete export report possible. This file will be named dump.dmp and will be written to your export folder; it can be reviewed using Notepad or whatever text editor you have to search for clues if problems arise with the export. Configuration Control is for saving your DTS export configuration information and has nothing to do with the config file you have to create in the export folder.

When you are ready to export the DTS file, click the Whole Shape button.

If you're not using the default player file but making an all-new player character, you'll want to export the DSQ animation files for each cycle of the animation process. This is done separately from the DTS file. To export animations, you'll want to delete your player mesh first (leaving the hierarchy of markers and biped animations) and click the Sequences button from the Torque DTS Exporter menu. Save it as a DSQ file with the name of the animation cycle (see the section "Embedding Animations" earlier in this chapter), such as player_forward.dsq. The default player biped we're using already has complete DSQ files in the data\shapes\player folder, so you won't have to re-create them.

Spotlight on Chronic Logic, LLC

Chronic Logic, LLC is a video game developer and publisher based in Santa Cruz, California. They develop and distribute indie games. Chronic Logic (see Figure 7.15) was founded by Alex Austin and Ben Nichols in 2001, just after Austin's Bridge Builder became popular. Later, Josiah Pisciotta joined the company. Nichols has since left Chronic Logic. I had a moment to talk to Josiah Pisciotta, who answered the following questions.

When did you first decide to use Torque to make a game, and what did you learn along the way?

Figure 7.15
The offices of Chronic Logic, LLC.

"I chose the Torque Game Engine in 2004 as my studio's game development platform for my current project. The key reasons were it had a proven working demo, an abundance of community-made resources, a large community and robust support forums, it runs on older computer specs, and the price was right. I had been toying with the free Torque demo since 2002. I bought my first license in 2003. Official production began on my current game on November 6, 2005. Having such a full-featured game development platform taught me how all the various components fit together and work. It was easy to get a grasp of the data structure. One can learn quite a bit by reading the commented code."

Were there any software limitations that had to be overcome or any special features that helped you out with Torque?

"Yes, there were limitations. I knew some things would not work right with how TGE is set up to work. The scope of our design did include some fairly heavy engine customizations. None of the limitations came as a surprise to us. No canned game engine solution is 100% perfect."

For a designer just starting out, is there any advice you can give?

"Yes

1. Design

First develop a rough idea. Then go and research the available technologies before you flesh out your designs or invest capital. Know that some things will be possible and some will not. I kept my design somewhat flexible where I was not 100% sure that the available technology would work or not, and I usually develop three to four contingency plans to cover those situations. Fully understand your technical limits and fight hard to work within them.

2. Pace

Second, be patient. Try to not rush things. Have deadlines, but don't let those make your game's quality and playability decisions. Take the time to read through your engine's code and learn as much as you can. Bounce ideas off non-game developers, like friends, family, or gamers. If you plan on selling your game, you will want it to appeal to as wide an audience as possible. Identify your market, and do some research on it. What are their buying patterns? Likes? Dislikes? What game did they buy last and why? This information should not drive your game's production, but it should be factored in.

3. Team

Third, find help. Build a solid core team. You probably won't be able to make a game on your own. If you can, you probably shouldn't. Two sets of eyes and opinions are better than one. Try and pair up with more specialized developers outside your specific field. Be a part of other game development projects. Serving on another developer's project will provide a real-world example of their successes and failures. See how development problems escalate and how they are solved. This will also give you a rough understanding of scheduling and managing talent. Take some time to know a bit about what each member of a development team does. Try and gain as much information as possible so you can speak intelligently on various subjects like programming, 3D/2D art, game design, audio, and production.

4. Develop

Fourth, understand what a good game developer does. Look at highly effective game developers and adopt similar traits. Look for industry models of success and try to learn from their examples or actions. You, after all, are developing a game.

5. Passion

Play as many PC/console games as you can get your hands on. Play games made with the D20 System. Play board and card games. Play games outside of your own personal interests. Demos are free and abundant.

Those are the points and rules I try to adhere to. For this younger audience I would like to add a few critical points:

Cater your education toward a game development track. If you are interested in programming, make sure you have the requirements met to follow a CS [computer science] degree. If your interest is art, take any game-related courses you can find, even 3D-application-specific courses and traditional media. Again, find a game project or game development studio and volunteer. Education is a huge part of being an effective game developer. Another large part is keeping up with the ever-changing technologies. Serving on a current project will let you apply what you have learned and give you a feel of how development technologies change.

The analogy I use is my own personal experience. What I learned in school was more or less hands-on history of game development. Serving on a few game projects was more like being on the front lines. Closer to the cutting edge. The best way to learn about cutting-edge game technologies is to be with the people inventing it."

What can we expect to see next from Chronic Logic?

"We are currently working on a patch as well as several retail publishing deals for our latest game *Kingdom Elemental* (see Figure 7.16). Our next game release will be our Torque-based game *Microwarrior*. We are also prototyping some smaller game ideas as side projects. We manage to stay very busy around here."

Figure 7.16
Kingdom Elemental (images courtesy of Chronic Logic, LLC, 2007).

Previewing Little Reaper in ShowTool Pro

The Torque ShowTool Pro, which is available on the companion CD, allows you to preview your game assets. Issues with the model, rigging, texture, and animation can be detected before importing the file into the Torque Game Engine. The image can be zoomed in, rotated, and re-lighted. You can preview your character in full animation by pressing the Play button. The animation loop can be played at full speed, slowed down, or scrolled through frame by frame.

Dealing with Problems

If you find any problems with your animation, you might not have exported correctly. You must check that every detail marker has a corresponding mesh object and that your mesh has no stray vertices. Re-read the tutorial, double-check the list of requirements before exporting, and if you still can't figure out the cause of the issue or you get a strange error message, you can look online at www.garagegames.com for possible answers.

Adding Levels of Detail

With 3ds Max, you can easily add LOD to your model, whether it's a vehicle, weapon, or prop item, by first applying the Multires modifier. Then you Clone the existing mesh shape two times, for a total of three shapes, and drop the Vertex Percentage for each of the meshes, starting with 100% and ending with 20%. Then you name each of the meshes with numbers at the end, like shape128, shape64, and shape2. You are also required to have dummy objects, like

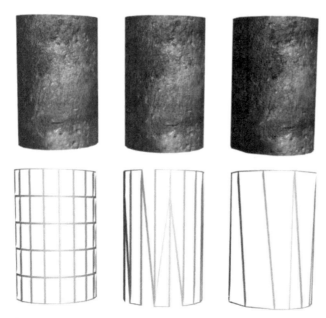

Figure 7.17
Shape128, shape64, and shape2.

detail128, detail64, and detail2, to correspond with your meshes for Torque to read them correctly. Your detail objects will be children of base01, while your shape128 will be the child of start01. Your shape128 will have the highest amount of detail, while your shape2 should have the least (see Figure 7.17). When you go into the DTS Exporter, have shape128 selected and click the Embed Shape button. The Exporter should auto-generate a hierarchy of levels of detail for you.

This means that whenever the character onscreen is seen at any size higher than 128 pixels, it will render as the most complex model, but as it gets farther away it will lose clarity, until it's only at 2 pixels and will have the most blurred shape. This saves the user a lot of rendering lag time and improves the graphic performance of your game.

Review

In this chapter you should have learned the following:

- What 3D models are good for in games.

- How to defeat real-time rendering issues by using low-poly modeling and LOD.

- How to come up with original game characters.

- What programs are good for creating DTS files.

- How to use 3ds Max 9 to create Torque game characters.

- How to build a model using box and segmented modeling.

- How to texture the model through UV mapping and UVW map editing.

- How to animate the model using the default player biped skeleton.

- How to export the model for use with Torque.

- How to preview the model in Torque ShowTool Pro and fix issues.

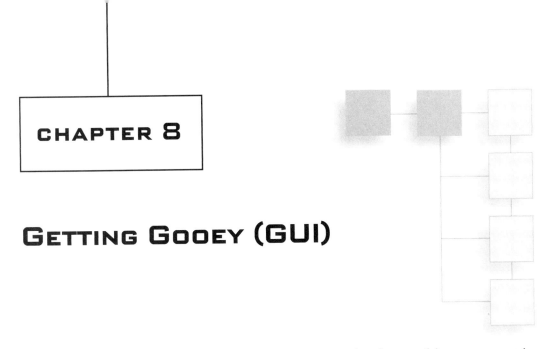

CHAPTER 8

GETTING GOOEY (GUI)

Before we talk about the GUI Editor, I want you to be thoroughly conversant in human-computer interface, or HCI. HCI determines the ease with which the end user of a computer program (in this case, the player who picks up your game) gets around and does what they want in the program itself. If you make the game controls too hard, your player will rebel. If it is difficult to move the character around or perform basic actions, then it is definitely not a fun game.

Games thrive or die by their controls. Games in which you cannot find your way through their maze of menus, or cannot get the character to go where you want, or cannot see the bad guys that are shooting at you—these games end up forgotten about in the bargain bins. Games that are easy and fun to play, while still offering unique challenges, last a long time and get talked about for years to come. You want your game to be one of the latter.

Human-Computer Interfaces

By "interface" we are talking about a two-way street, a phone call, or a translator between two diplomats. Two individuals are communicating back and forth to reach a conclusion. A human-computer interface, alternatively mammal-machine interaction (isn't that cute?), involves a human and a computer trying to reach a mutual conclusion, and the translator between the two is the interface.

Think about it. When you start up a game on your Xbox or PlayStation, you are greeted by the preset menu options that typically let you start a new game, load a saved game, edit settings, or give you some other option. Once you have started the game, you can open other menus, control your onscreen character, and save your game. All of these are interfaces that have to be programmed by the game's designers so that you can enjoy the game.

Input/Output

Essentially, these interfaces break down into two tasks:

- **Input**—You tell the computer what you want to do.

- **Output**—The computer reacts based on its programming.

Input/Output, or I/O, is a concept that is really very easy to understand. While you are telling the programming what you want to do (such as load, save, or pick up ammo), the programming has to respond to what you tell it. Most of the time an interface uses the mouse and keyboard or, in the case of console games, the peripherals rest on the game controller.

Emergent Gameplay

Before you get excited about programming complex game environments that adapt to the player, such as in games like *Fable* and *Grand Theft Auto,* there is an underlying principle you must understand called *emergent gameplay.*

Emergent gameplay comes about not so much from what you set up or program into your game but what you don't! Gamers play the game's underlying program, not the game story, remember? Gamers who are really good will set up situational challenges for themselves in your game levels that you will never predict. Your job is to try to predict this type of play and offer an invisible guiding hand.

For instance, the stealth game *Thief: Deadly Shadows* (see Figure 8.1) has you playing Garrett, a cat burglar in moonlit medieval settings. Your mission is spelled out for you in each of the levels. Your challenge is getting it done. The real fun comes in emergent gameplay because you can make up how you approach a problem as you play the game.

One of the first missions has you breaking into a nobleman's mansion to steal an opal. You can choose to quench the flame in a sculpture outside, which alerts a

Figure 8.1
Thief: Deadly Shadows (image courtesy of Eidos, 2004).

cook informant on the inside who will open a small door for you in the parapet. You could also sneak around to a side window and climb in there. You could also knock out the guards and walk right past their unconscious forms. Whatever you decide to do, the designers set up the scenario and let you have fun your own way! The mission never changes, but the way you achieve it is dependent on your actions.

Usability

Tip

"Interface design is an excellent proving ground for gameplay features. After you have an idea for a new feature (or an improvement upon an existing one), consider how the interface will work. If you can't come up with a seamless interface, you should seriously consider abandoning or redesigning the feature."

—Kevin Saunders, Obsidian Entertainment

Besides considering how a game will react to the player's choices, and taking into account emergent gameplay, you must also learn what truly makes a great interface, regardless of whether you're designing a great game or not. Computer science professor Ben Schneiderman, who wrote *Designing the User Interface: Strategies for Effective Human-Computer Interaction* (Addison-Wesley, 1997), has a list of principles that should be included behind every system interface you design:

1. **Strive for consistency**—If you always keep a command button in one place, don't have it drift anywhere else. If you're designing a computer game, the nearly universal controls for character movement are going to be W, A, S, and D or the arrow keys. Don't change it.

2. **Enable frequent users to adopt their own shortcuts**—Letting players learn macros or develop their own hotkeys won't make your game suffer. It will only help.

3. **Offer informative feedback**—This goes right back to the lesson on the Four Fs of Great Game Design (Fun, Fairness, Feedback, and Feasibility).

4. **Design dialogues to yield closure**—When the player finishes saving her game, you ought to let her know it was saved successfully.

5. **Offer simple error handling**—If there is an error, let the user know what kind.

6. **Permit easy reversal of actions**—Games usually don't have an Undo command, but if the player's character dies he should be able to go back to a checkpoint or a previously saved game. Make it easy on players if they mess up.

7. **Reduce short-term memory load**—Doing this can sometimes be difficult, but try to keep your file sizes low and purge assets you aren't using at the time so your engine runs smoothly. The Torque engine is really good about handling memory resources.

The most important lesson of all when designing a user interface is that any element left open for interpretation will almost always return erroneous results.

This is one of the reasons why a lot of games have similar kinds of controls and similar menus. You might occasionally see different descriptive words, like using "Run Away" instead of "Quit Game," but the two are very close and the reader will still know what you mean.

If you ever make a game so complicated that players can't jump right into it and start playing without first having to stop and read a walkthrough or manual, then just shoot your dreams down right now. You want to design a game that players can sit down and find themselves completely immersed in within just a few minutes. The turning point for this is designing a great game interface.

Graphical User Interface (GUI)

GUI design is an important adjunct to software. Its goal is to enhance the usability of a program. GUIs include graphic elements called *widgets* that the user manipulates to interact with the program. The most common widgets used on computers today are windows, buttons, icons, menus, scroll bars, pointers, and pop-up windows. A game GUI may consist of both the out-of-game menu system and the in-game displays for health, ammo, points scored, or whatever else your particular game might need.

You don't have to be a great artist to design perfect GUIs, but it never hurts. Most GUIs used for games look approximately the same. Part of the reason artists make them similar to each other is for familiarity, which adds to the GUI's usability. So if you are unsure how to make your GUIs look or how your controls should act, look at other games in the same genre.

Tip

"All the components of an interface are equally important. It is like a symphony orchestra. If the performance is to be effective, all instruments must be in tune and all notes must be played correctly. If the interface is to be successful, all components must work together."

—Jan McWilliams, Director of Interactive Design Art Institute of California, Los Angeles

GUI Editor

As mentioned in Chapter 2, "The Torque Game Engine," the GUI Editor is part of the WYSIWYG (what-you-see-is-what-you-get) system Torque gives you to speed your game development. The GUI Editor's major intent lies in you designing the interface for your game. Using the drag-and-drop creator, you can put together any interface that you want for your game. The GUI Editor provides you with many prefab controls and the ability to create new controls based on your own scripting.

Under the Hood of the GUI Editor

YournameDemo still opens to the FPS Starter Kit menu. As a brief introduction to the GUI Editor, we are going to change that. The GUI Editor can get hairy pretty quickly if you don't pay close attention to what you are doing or what you have just done. It is also fairly easy to hose your interface if you're not careful, so it comes as a strong recommendation to save your interface often.

GUI Editor Displays

From the FPS Starter Kit menu screen, select the GUI Editor (F10). The editor starts with the GUI currently loaded, which in this case is the standard Torque start screen. The interface (see Figure 8.2) should be pretty familiar to you. It is similar to the World Editor: there is a window on the right with a tree list on top containing hierarchical information and the GUI Inspector on the bottom with data pertaining to the object selected. Take a moment to look at some of the items on the tree and click on them to see their properties in the Inspector.

Figure 8.2
The GUI Editor.

There are three drop-down buttons just below the menu, and each one has a drop-down list that pops up when you click on it.

- **New Control**—Displays a list of all controls from which the user can select to add to the current content.

- **Show GUI**—Displays the name of the interface (GUI) currently being edited. Notice that you're already in MainMenuGui. If you switch to another GUI while in the middle of editing another, you might have trouble saving the other GUI.

- **Virtual Screen Size**—This sets the screen size resolution. Select 640 × 480, and then go to 1024 × 768 before returning to where you started, just to get the hang of this.

Changing the Background

From the CD, copy and paste projects\Chapter 8\welcomeBG.jpg to Yourname Demo\client\ui. This is the main folder for all your GUI files. If you want to add your own personal touch to this background, you can open welcomeBG.jpg in an image editing program. For one thing, you can write ''This Game Created by . . .'' and put in your name. Later, when you create other games, you can make the background look like anything you want.

Back in the GUI Editor, select the MainMenuGui in the tree list. In the Inspector, find the Misc section and the Bitmap field. Press the browse button to change the file name from the current background image file to welcomeBG.jpg (which you just placed in the client\ui folder). If nothing happens, hit Apply to see the change take effect. You should see that you have a new background, this one with the *Abandon All Hope* title.

Editing Widgets

Click on Recordings and hit Delete. You can click on the other buttons and see what they do. They tell you that if you scroll down through their list of attributes, you'll find Parent > Command. This is where a part of the script is called whenever the button is clicked. Don't delete any more buttons, as we might still be able to use the rest of them.

You should see something close to Figure 8.3. This is suitable for our purposes.

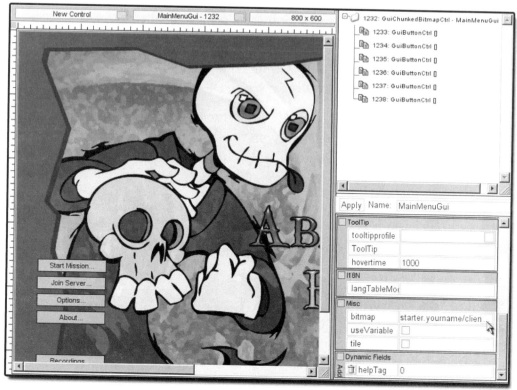

Figure 8.3
Adding a new background.

Click on the Start Mission button. Scroll through its available attributes on the right to find Misc > Text, and you'll see the text for the Start Mission button. Highlight the words "Start Mission," and type **Play Game**. Hit Apply to see your text on the button. Click-drag the selected control on the GUI screen over and under the game title (where it says *Abandon All Hope*). For more accurate nudging, you can use the arrow keys to move the control incrementally left, right, up, and down one pixel at a time. (Optionally, you can hold down Shift and use the arrow keys to move the control ten pixels at a time.) Use the control's guidelines for accurate placement. To scale the selected control, you can grab it

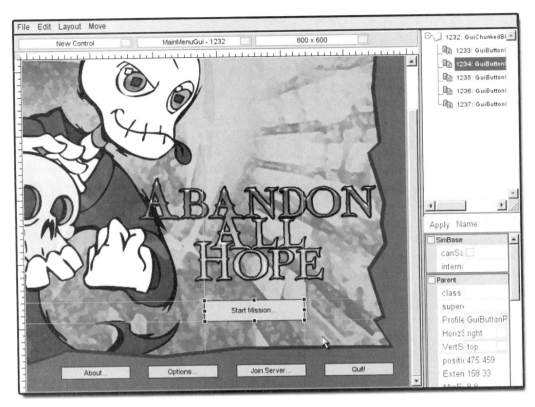

Figure 8.4
Placing the widgets where you want them.

with your cursor by one of its handles and drag the handle to resize its appearance.

You can also move the remaining buttons to the bottom of the screen, under the picture. If you want to select more than one button at once, you'll notice that the eight squares surrounding each control will turn pure white. This means that you can no longer resize any of the controls, but you can drag them and align them at will.

When you are through, your GUI should look similar to Figure 8.4.

Adding a Widget

The New Control drop-down button under the menu bar contains options for creating new widgets, which help the user control the game through the interface that you're building. All of the buttons you see in the GUI already are from the

Figure 8.5
Inserting a new widget.

control type GuiButtonCtrl. You can add a new GuiButtonCtrl from the New Control drop-down list. Your new button will appear in the upper-left corner of the GUI, as seen in Figure 8.5.

In the Inspector, go to Misc > Text and type the text you want to appear on your new button. It can say anything you like. Just telling the user that the widget says something does not actually make the game do that something, however. If you want the button to do something when clicked, you have to add a command to the widget. You do that in the Parent > Command field. However, you have to type a legitimately scripted command.

Depending on what screen resolution you're in when you place a widget, the widget will only look good when you are viewing the GUI at that screen resolution. To fix this, select your widget, then scroll through the Inspector until you find horizSizing and vertSizing and change them both to Relative, then hit Apply. Check your screen size by flipping between 640 × 480 and 1024 × 768 (see Figure 8.6). If you see any detail you missed, or if any element looks wrong at a different size, you need to go back and change its attributes before moving on.

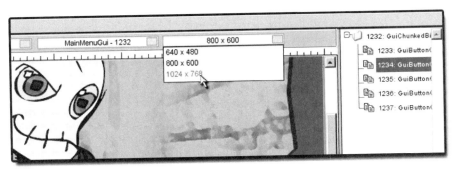

Figure 8.6
Changing the screen resolution.

Saving Your GUI

To save your GUI, select File > Save GUI, and save it to YournameDemo\
client\ui. You can exit the GUI Editor by pressing F10. When you re-enter
Torque, you will see your brand-spanking-new start screen. Press the Play Game
button, and your first game level should start. When you press the Quit button, it
should exit. If it doesn't, or if nothing happens when you press on the buttons, go
back to the GUI Editor and see if there's a problem with the file path or something else that you might've missed.

Play Game

Right now we still have a problem. The player will open our new start screen, but
if he clicks on Play Game, it will take him to the old FPS Starter Kit mission
choice screen. It's easy for us to open up the mission we've been editing from
inside the Torque Editor, but we want to fix it so that the player will come to our
level right away without getting lost.

Open main.cs from the YournameDemo folder. Scroll down to the very bottom
and input this code snippet:

```
// LOAD MY MISSION
function loadMyMission()
{
  // make sure we are not connected to a server already
  disconnect();
  // Create the server and load the mission
  createServer("SinglePlayer",
expandFilename("./data/missions/YournameDemoMission.mis"));
  // Make a local connection
  %conn = new GameConnection(ServerConnection);
```

```
RootGroup.add(ServerConnection);
%conn.setConnectArgs("Player");
%conn.setJoinPassword("None");
%conn.connectLocal();
}
```

Where it says "YournameDemoMission.mis," type in the name of the mission that you've been creating and editing from scratch, as this is the game level you want your players to play. Save main.cs and launch YournameDemo. Press F10 to enter the GUI Editor and, on the main start screen, click on the Play Game button. Scroll through this button's attributes on the lower-right of your screen to find Command. Highlight the original command and type this into the field:

```
loadMyMission();
```

Your screen should look like Figure 8.7. Click Apply and save your GUI (remember that this GUI was named MainMenuGui) to overwrite the old one with your changes. Then test it out.

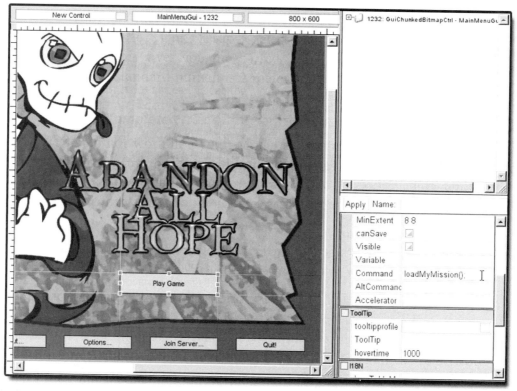

Figure 8.7
Changing the button to start your own game mission.

Aligning Multiple Widgets

You can align your new buttons anywhere on the screen that you want without click-dragging them there. The following hotkeys are the ones you use to align multiple controls to the screen:

- **Align Left**—Moves the selected controls all the way to the left to line up with the left-most control [CTRL+L (Win) or CMD+L (Mac)].
- **Align Right**—Moves the selected controls all the way to the right to line up with the right-most control [CTRL+R (Win) or CMD+R (Mac)].
- **Align Top**—Moves the selected controls all the way to the top to line up with the top-most control [CTRL+T (Win) or CMD+T (Mac)].
- **Align Bottom**—Moves the selected controls all the way to the bottom to line up with the bottom-most control [CTRL+B (Win) or CMD+B (Mac)].

You can also align your widgets using the Layout menu, which features the above commands as well as others that don't have specific hotkeys.

- **Center Horizontally**—Moves the selected controls all the way to the center to line up horizontally.
- **Space Horizontally**—Moves the selected controls out horizontally to line up in a row.
- **Space Vertically**—Moves the selected controls out vertically to line up in a row.
- **Bring to Front**—Raises a control above another in stacking order.
- **Send to Back**—Puts a control below another in stacking order.

Adding a Score Counter

You have learned how to create a menu element, basically just a widget, for the start screen. There are lots of other widgets you could add to the start screen, which you can experiment with on your own time. You can also create in-game interfaces, which can display the player's ammo, life, health status, score, or other important information.

We're going to create a score counter for your game to show you how in-game GUIs work. The Little Reaper is going to run around in the game level and try to catch as many Skulls as possible, right? We need to set up a score counter that shows how many Skulls the Little Reaper has caught.

The quickest way to open a GUI for an in-game interface is to exit the GUI Editor (F10) and enter your game. Once in the game, you can press F10 again to open the GUI Editor, and you should see that PlayGui, the default GUI selected when inside a game, is selected in the drop-down list under GUIs to edit. If you don't

Figure 8.8
Pick GuiTextCtrl from the New Control drop-down list.

want to take that route, you can always pick PlayGui from the drop-down list, as long as you're not in the middle of editing another GUI.

Select GuiTextCtrl from the New Control drop-down list (see Figure 8.8). Make sure that your new control is in the tree list to the right and that it is selected so that its attributes show up in the Inspector on the bottom right. It might be a good idea, since we'll do some scripting, to name this widget. In the empty text field next to the Apply button, type **SkullCounter**. Notice that I did not put any spaces or strange wildcard characters in this name. When you give a specific object a name so the object can be controlled in TorqueScript, you should never put any spaces or wildcard characters in the name, or else you'll probably hose the engine. So be careful what you type for its name. Also, it's smart to write the name down so that you can refer to it later without having to backtrack to find out what it was called.

Figure 8.9
Your score counter.

Scroll down to Parent > Profile. Click the browse button beside GuiTextProfile to select GuiBigTextProfile. GuiBigTextProfile is a standard format used for big letters to show up onscreen.

Go to the General section and enter **Skulls: 0** in the text field and then hit Apply. Your Skulls: 0 should appear on the screen in big letters (see Figure 8.9). Move it wherever you want and test it at the different screen sizes to see what it looks like; if you think it looks wonky at another screen size, remember to change HorizSizing and VertSizing to Relative.

When you're satisfied with how the score counter looks, select File > Save GUI and save your GUI as YournameDemo\client\ui\playGui.gui. We'll have to do some actual scripting to get the score counter to work, but otherwise you're done.

Editing Existing GUI Elements

If you want to edit the default healthbar image, you can find it in the client\ui folder. It is called healthBar.png. The ui folder has most of the default GUI elements for your editing pleasure. Customizing existing game parts often makes for a better game. Just make sure that your end product remains consistent with the original concept and theme of your game.

Review

After reading this chapter, you should know the following:

- What human-computer interfaces, or HCI, are all about.

- What the rules of usability are and how emergent gameplay is a part of game interfaces.

- How to open the GUI Editor.

- How to edit an existing GUI.

- How to change the start screen's background image.

- How to create new controls, or widgets.

- How to manipulate and add commands to new controls, or widgets.

- How to create an in-game interface, such as a score counter.

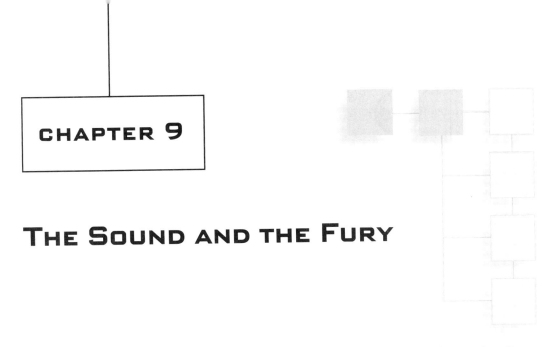

CHAPTER 9

THE SOUND AND THE FURY

Humans are an amazing bunch. We can perceive auditory signals coming from many different directions at once and singularly separate the sounds based on where they come from. Sound forms at least a full one-fifth of the way we perceive our environment, and we innately use sound as a means of survival. Being capable of telling when a noisy ambush predator like a cougar snuck up behind our ancestors helped them stay alive—and today we use sound to listen to the latest pop hits on our MP3 players.

Sound makes everything come alive. It stamps the heartbeat for our culture and provides us with an aural experience. It can support the story of a game and shape the soundtrack. Try playing a video game with the TV or the computer speakers on mute. Watch a YouTube video without headphones or a speaker, and you'll realize just how disappointing the experience quickly becomes.

We are going to look at how you create sound for use with Torque, and you'll learn to edit sound using Audacity.

Sound Used in TV and Film

Electronic games follow the cinematic wake of the TV and movie industry, so game designers can learn a lot from the way those industries use sound. Sound can support a narrative, documentary, or commercial film or program, telling the story directly or indirectly and enhancing the overall experience.

A Short History Lesson

The movie industry started seriously using sound in the 1920s, but the process was incredibly difficult back then. Because of limitations to the sound cameras, actors often had to be experienced theatrical performers and practically shout to be heard on the final recording. A good deal of silent film actors lost their jobs at this time because audiences discovered many of them had poor speaking voices or foreign accents.

Today's recording processes are a lot better, and most of the work goes straight to digital tracks. Actors can act naturally and underplay their roles if they wish and still be heard in the final edit. Unfortunately, directors are becoming more and more lackadaisical and put a lot of technical problems on the sound engineers. They are expected to make actors' voices sound clear in post-production, even if the directors can't hear them on set.

The people working on the production of a film or TV show think of sound every step of the way. Screenplay writers make suggestions for noises that may be heard and lines of dialogue to be spoken by paid actors. Location scouts consider noise conditions of prospective shooting sites. Though directors can frame a shot to effectively remove a sign or offensive place from being seen on camera, they have no control over random noises, such as airplanes flying overhead or construction workers off-camera.

Sound delivery has also improved vastly over the years. Sound delivery started out mono, and only as recently as the 1970s went to stereo. Today's modern audiences, including you, not only expect to hear their TV shows, movies, and games in stereo, they expect to be rocked by Dolby surround sound and amplified bass. The increased resolution of HDTV images requires a similarly improved high-definition sound track. A 5.1 high-fidelity surround-sound system, which literally surrounds you with the best sound, provides the most balanced aesthetic energy between picture and sound. The technology has advanced, and even the game industry must stop and think about sound critically during development.

Hyper-Real Sound

You may not realize it, but most film and TV sound for your entertainment pleasure does not come from the original recorded sound. Sounds you hear in cinema are rarely accurate representations of real sounds.

Instead, engineers construct the sound in post-production, utilizing many pieces of sound they mix together in software programs to create a seamless whole. These professionals often take separate pieces from sound effects libraries and custom recordings done in studios, what's called *Foley sound*. Foley artists record custom sound effects that emphasize sounds that should be heard in context. For instance, a Foley artist might shake a sheet of metal to record thunder or squash melons to represent a character getting squished by a falling anvil.

When creating a game, every piece of sound has to be manipulated by the game programmer, and the piece of sound used can be hyper-real, placing emphasis that subtly influences the game's players.

Sound Fundamentals

The Greek mathematician Pythagoras not only delivered us a triangle but also discovered the octave and came up with numeric ratios connected to harmony. Galileo formed many of the scientific laws of sound. Since the 1600s there have been numerous advances in the study of sound, some of them coming from such great individuals as Heinrich Hertz (where we get "Hertz" from) and Alexander Graham Bell (where we get "decibel" from).

Sound comes in the shape of vibration waves. Some sound waves can actually travel at frequencies so high or low that humans cannot hear them, but some animals can (such as a dog hearing a dog whistle).

Here are some of the most basic laws of sound:

- A sound wave moves pretty much in a straightforward fashion.

- *Pitch* refers to how fast the sound wave vibrates, also known as *frequency*. Humans can discern sound frequencies by a 2:1 difference, so many of our music notes are on a scale of 2.

- The term *Hertz* (Hz) comes from a unit of frequency equaling one vibration per second.

- *Intensity* is how loud the sound comes across, also called *amplitude* or *volume*. Intensity can be measured by the decibel, or dB. The increasing intensity of a sound wave is known as *gain*.

■ *Timbre* is the waveform or accuracy of the sound frequency. Timbre is different for every instrument and every voice, and it reflects a change in quality that is not dependent on intensity or frequency.

Influencing Factors

The outside factors that influence sound include space, time, situation, and outside events. As with many of the other elements of media aesthetics, these factors can overlap.

Space

Location defines many sounds. Stereo sound makes it possible to hear sound relative to onscreen positioning. For instance, most of the player character's dialogue will come from the front forward-facing speaker in 5.1 Dolby surround sound, but if you show a comrade yelling for the player to catch up and you show him slightly off-screen over on the right, you best make sure the sound comes out of the right-side speakers.

Sound perspective means that you must also match close-up video images with "near" sounds, and long shots with sounds that come from far away. Close sounds take the spotlight, often sharing more presence than the softer background noises. The same principle takes the Doppler effect (see Figure 9.1) from physics to media: as a loud sound source comes closer to the listener, the higher the sound gains; the farther away the sound source moves from the listener, the

Figure 9.1
An illustration of the Doppler effect.

softer the sound gets until it fades completely. Positioning themselves in a virtual world, 3D sounds take advantage of the Doppler effect. In most 3D game engines, this is handled for you if you use 3D sound (more on this later in this chapter).

Time

Different times of the day and different climates are reflected in sound. If you are creating a summer glen, you will want to use noises such as chirping birds, breezes blowing, or tree branches rustling. On the other hand, a scene that takes place at night might have owls hooting, crickets chirping, or coyotes barking in the distance.

There are two special uses of sound that have to do with time.

Predictive Sound

Predictive sound involves the placement of certain sounds before an event actually takes place. An example of a predictive sound would be letting the player of a game hear battle sounds coming from over a hill before showing him that there is a fight taking place or letting the player hear a rumbling noise right before an earthquake shakes the streets his character's walking down.

Leitmotiv

The other special use of sound dealing with time is the *leitmotiv* (German for "leading motif"). Some games play a short music piece every time a specific boss monster or enemy shows up, letting the player know that she has to prepare to fight. The leitmotiv most often heard in the popular survival horror games under the *Resident Evil* title is the moaning of zombies, as seen but not really heard in Figure 9.2. If the player enters a room or new area, she doesn't even have to see a shambling corpse; if she can hear a shuffling noise or a low moan, she knows she's about to have to face off against the undead.

Situations and Outside Events

Sounds can describe a specific situation or (used cleverly) be effected by outside events that help put the listener into the scene.

Here is one example: A lonely geezer leaves the front door of his wooden shack high in the snow-capped mountains to chop wood. He crunches through snow with every step, and occasionally the forest is disturbed by the cries of hawks; but otherwise the sound stays very much muted. Why, you might ask? Snow acts as a

Figure 9.2
The shuffling of zombies is a big indicator of danger around the next corner (*Resident Evil 5,* image courtesy of Konami, 2007).

sort of natural sound dampener, absorbing noises. So the scene would be a hushed one.

Starting Your Own Sound Studio

There are some serious fundamentals to starting a home studio space that you must keep in mind. You will probably set up your recording studio around your computer desk, in your bedroom or garage. The garage might be best, simply because of the sound isolation there. We will discuss the two most important aspects to remember when setting up your own sound studio—soundproofing and setup—and then we'll look at what it takes to start recording.

Soundproofing

Make sure that the room you use does not have serious leaks where sound can invade, such as door cracks and windows. You will want to keep outside noise from filtering in, and you want to stop short of being a nuisance to your parents and neighbors. Sound absorption and isolation will be your primary goals.

Short of going out and buying expensive commercial eggshell panels to cover the walls and ceiling in your room or garage, you can drape wool blankets over the windows and door or add bookshelves filled with books to your walls. This will limit the amount of reflective sound (or echoing) while improving the sound quality when you record. You might also make sure that your parents, siblings, or pets know you are recording before you start so they won't walk in and disturb you in the middle of a complicated recording session.

Setup

You will need an easy-to-use sound editing software program to do audio mixes with, and if the program you choose does not include a recording or micro-phone-line-in system, you might have to use Microsoft's built-in sound recorder or another inexpensive software to initially record your audio. The following programs are the most widely used sound mixing packages and their prices at the time of this printing:

- **Audacity**—free

- **NCH Swift Sound**—free

- **Cool Edit Pro/Adobe Audition**—$349

- **Soundtrack Pro 2**—$1,299 (Mac only)

- **SLab**—free (Linux only)

- **Cakewalk's SONAR Home Studio**—$139

- **Sound Forge Audio Studio**—$59.95

Before using a sound editing program, you should check to make sure that your computer has a suitable sound card and peripheral speakers for playback. Besides having the right computer software and hardware, you must also have a micro-phone. There are fundamentally two different types of microphones to choose from: dynamic and condenser microphones.

Dynamic microphones use a wire coil over a magnet to catch sound waves, producing an electronic voltage in response to sound. These microphones reproduce sound pretty well, but their accuracy is based on voltage rather than the sound source.

For killer vocal recording, you should consider a condenser microphone. Con-denser microphones use an electronically charged stretched diaphragm over a thin plate, and fluctuations caused by sound waves passing over the diaphragm cause changes in the electronic current, producing output signals. Condenser microphones tend to be more accurate than dynamic microphones, particularly in mid and high frequencies. Unfortunately they are more fragile and less likely to handle abuse.

Practice will show you whether or not you have chosen the right sound editing setup for your needs. Practice with your microphone to see what its sound range is like and if you pick up any background noise. If your microphone is sensitive enough to pick up the fan motor on your computer, you might have to replace the fan motor on your computer or tone the mic's sensitivity down a notch. Practice with recording techniques until you find the right setup that works for you.

Sound Recording

If you plan on recording your own voice, you must stop and think about your voice, how you place the microphone, and how to mix digital audio files on the computer.

Listen to Yourself

Evaluate how you sound on the mic. The human voice is a complex topic in and of itself. There are many tricks to make you sound better. The majority of these tricks to consider are as follows.

Posture

Stand or sit up straight. Let your muscles in your body relax. Don't let tension build up, or it will tighten your vocal cords. Don't slump down in your chair or lean way over when talking.

Remember to Breathe

Breathing is critical to enunciation. Unless you practice breathing correctly, you can develop poor habits that make your speech pattern erratic, soft, or breathless. You should take deep breaths in, letting them out slowly, to practice proper breathing. Don't take up smoking or hollering your lungs out when you have a chest cold, because you can actually hurt your organs.

Don't Crack Up

If you talk so loud or so fast that your voice actually cracks, you are "craking up," and it won't sound good. Breaks—or noticeable pauses or transitions in your speech—will maintain a more consistent sound. Knowing when to take breaks will increase your overall performance and, if you time them well, will give your listeners a more pleasurable experience.

Say It, Don't Spray It

Your unique tone, the speed with which you speak, how clearly you speak, and the interplay of your expression with the words you are reading—these are the most critical elements in making you an effective speaker. Part of your delivery comes from the words you are speaking, and part of your delivery comes from how you speak them. You have a unique vibe all your own. Strive to be yourself, but do so in a way that others can understand your message.

Digital Sound

It is important before we get started mixing and using digital audio files in the Torque Game Engine to understand what digital sound files are called, what compression of these files is all about, and some of the most basic keywords in digital sound mixing.

Sound File Formats

Computer-based sound editing generally involves one of three digital audio file formats: WAV files, MP3 files, and OGG files. WAV files are uncompressed, while MP3 and OGG files are compressed.

WAV Files   WAV files are usually uncompressed audio files. This means that they can be quite large and sound pretty good. The quality of a WAV file is determined by how well it was originally recorded or converted. Generally, you will want to work with WAV files for some sounds, but they can take up quite a lot of room in memory.

Compressed Files   Compression restricts the range of sound by attenuating signals exceeding a threshold. By attenuating louder signals, you limit the dynamic range of sound to existing signals. Imagine that the audio file is a piece of paper with sheet notes on it. Compressing it is literally wadding up the piece of paper into a tiny ball. To listen to the music in its compressed state, you have to use a device like an MP3 player to un-wad and smooth out the piece of paper. The most popular compressed audio file on the market right now (mostly due to the popularity of iPods and other MP3 players) is the MP3.

MP3 stands for Moving Pictures Expert Group, Audio Layer 3. It started in the 1980s by the German Fraunhofer Institut. In 1997, the first commercially acceptable MP3 player was created, called the AMP MP3 Playback Engine, which was later cloned into the more popular Winamp software by college students Justin Frankel and Dmitry Boldyrev. Napster and its gangbuster follow-up MP3 file-sharing services blew the lid off the MP3 boom, making it the number one most-recognized audio file on the Internet.

For other systems, Ogg Vorbis is probably the format of choice on Linux systems and AIFF for Macintosh. OGG files use a different (and some say better) encoding process to compress the audio. If you've never heard of OGG files before, check out www.vorbis.com for more information.

Audacity

A great open-source program (meaning it doesn't cost you anything under the GNU General Public License) is Audacity. It's the program suggested for you to use and is enclosed on the book's CD. Go ahead and install your free Audacity on your machine, if you haven't already, and we'll look at how you use it.

Recording

Let's record some sound. Open up Audacity and click the Record button, as shown in Figure 9.3. The program is now recording from your microphone, so you better say something. You can see the progress and the waveforms of the sounds in the Audacity window as you speak.

When you're through talking, click the Stop button. Play back your recording by clicking the Play button. If you can't hear anything coming out, but you see a waveform in Audacity, make sure you have the volume turned up on your computer and your speakers. If everything looks good, but you still can't hear any sound, check the microphone level in the Mixer Control in Audacity, and you might raise it a notch. Other things that can go wrong include using a bad mic, having the mic plugged into the wrong slot in your sound card, or the sound recording or playback volume defaulting to mute. Before panicking, make sure to check each of these things.

Editing

Now, if you didn't start speaking into the mic right away, you will probably have a long period of "dead air" before the sound wave you made and another chunk

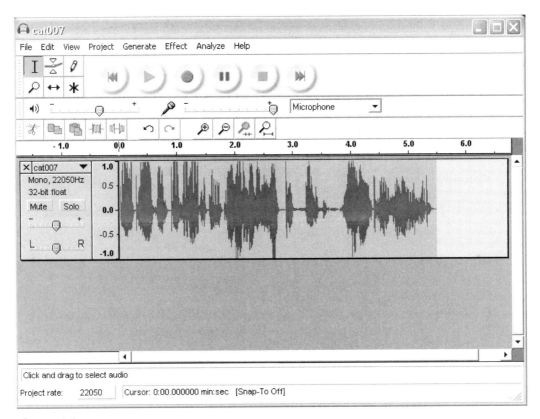

Figure 9.3
Recording with Audacity.

of "dead air" after. This is typical, but it's certainly not optimal for a sound you're recording for a game. You have to edit your sound.

Place your cursor at one side of the portion of the waveform you wish to get rid of and drag it across to the other side, highlighting the area you want eliminated. Then go to Edit > Delete. The selected portion will be removed from the waveform. Notice under the Edit menu that you also have the option to Cut and Paste, which will come in handy when you are mixing multiple sound tracks.

Play back the audio to make sure you didn't remove too much or not enough of the waveform. Eventually, you'll have it finished.

Effects

I suggest you highlight the entire waveform and experiment with the effects that ship with Audacity. Click on the Effect menu to pick and play around with any of these effects, and you can play back the sound to hear how each effect changes the recording. When you find an effect you don't like, you can select Edit > Undo to remove it. Following is a list of effects you can try:

- **Repeat**—Repeats the last effect command.

- **Amplify**—Increases or decreases the volume of your track.

- **Bass Boost**—Amplifies the lower frequencies, leaving the other frequencies untouched.

- **Change Pitch**—Changes the audio pitch without affecting the tempo.

- **Change Speed**—Resamples and changes the speed, thereby changing the pitch.

- **Change Tempo**—Changes the tempo (speed) of the audio without affecting the pitch.

- **Click Removal**—Removes clicks, pops, and other artifact noises.

- **Compressor**—Compresses the range of the audio so the louder parts are quieter.

- **Echo**—Repeats the audio again and again, softer each time, like an echo.

- **Equalization**—Amplifies or diminishes specified frequencies using curves.

- **Fade In/Out**—Fades audio in or out.

- **FFT Filter**—Applies a Fast Fourier Transform using a curve on a linear scale.

- **Invert**—Flips the audio upside down.

- **Noise Removal**—Removes constant background noise, such as the wind, fans, tape noise, or humming.

- **Normalize**—Corrects for vertical (DC) offset of the signal.

- **Nyquist Prompt**—Uses a programming language to massage the audio.

- **Phaser**—Combines phase-shifted signals with the original.

- **Repeat**—Repeats the audio a given number of times.

- **Reverse**—This makes the audio run backwards, which is really cool!

- **Wahwah**—Uses a moving bandpass filter to create a wah-wah sound over the existing signal.

Exporting

Lastly, you need to save the bit of dialogue or sound effect as a file so you can use it in Torque. Go to File > Export as WAV and name your file trialrun.wav, putting it somewhere convenient for the moment, such as your Desktop. Browse to your Desktop or wherever you placed the file, and double-click (Win) or single-click (Mac) to open it in your operating system's default media player. Listen to your sound as it exists.

Note

You have to find a special plug-in to export your recordings as compressed MP3 files. As this is not really necessary for our current game project, the MP3 encoder is not found on the CD; but you can do a brief Web search to discover it.

Sounds in the Torque Game Engine

You can record, edit, and export sounds using Audacity, but once you have the digital audio files ready, you have to know the correct way to plug them into Torque to make them work in your game. We'll look at how Torque handles sound, and then you'll put your recorded sounds into your game to test them out.

Sound Support in Torque

The Torque Game Engine uses OpenAL for sound support, plus you can look online for further resources to use alternative libraries. Sound is one area that TGE makes look difficult at first, but it turns out to be much easier in execution. Sound support is handled by the following three devices:

- Audio descriptions (or ADs)

- Audio profiles (or APs)

- Console functions

2D and 3D Sounds

TGE supports what are called 2D and 3D sounds. Torque separates these two classifications by whether or not the sounds have a source in the game world. Let's take a closer look at this definition.

2D Sound

Two-dimensional sound has no auditory source in the game environment, which means there's no object in your game world that pushes the sound. 2D sound gain is not attenuated by orientation, spatial placement, or position. The majority of 2D sounds that you hear in games include the following:

- Start-up or intro music

- Background (soundtrack) music

- Menu interface beeps and clicks

- Short-call noises (like cheering crowds or cries of dismay)

- Universal environment sounds (such as roaring winds or crowd noises)

3D Sound

3D sounds have a defined position, place, and source somewhere in the game environment. They come from somewhere and players can hear them getting louder the closer the players move to them, then the sounds lose gain as players get farther away from them. 3D sounds make full use of the Doppler effect. Most of the 3D sounds you hear in games include the following:

- The player character's footfalls, grunts, and cries of pain

- Moving vehicle noises

- Weapons fire and explosions

- Local environment sounds (such as a bubbling river, roaring waterfall, or a cloud of flies)

Sound Channels

TGE comes with certain sound channels, which are often dedicated to certain tasks. It is recommended that you not switch or change these channels but rather add new ones as you need them. The preset TGE channels are as follows:

- **Channel 0**—$DefaultAudioType

- **Channel 1**—$GuiAudioType

- **Channel 2**—$SimAudioType

AudioDescriptions (ADs)

Throughout the scripting for TGE, you will need to place certain fields of code that encapsulate sound-specific data to simplify the programming. Audio-Description datablocks define how a sound is set up and how it plays.

The AudioDescription datablock tells the computer whether the sound is meant to be 2D or 3D, and, if it is 3D, what sound cones it has. It also tells the computer if the sound is meant to loop, and if so how many times it loops. Lastly, the AudioDescription sets up the maximum gain (or how loud the sound can get) and what channel the sound should play on. Remember, it is recommended to set new sound channels rather than overwrite existing ones.

The following is an example of an AudioDescription datablock:

```
datablock AudioDescription ( YourGameNonLooping3DADDB ) {
volume = 1.0;
isLooping = false;
is3D = true;
ReferenceDistance = 2.0;
MaxDistance = 25.0;
type = $SimAudioType;
};
```

This AudioDescription datablock creates a uniquely named sound named YourGameNonLooping3DADDB, which is a non-looping 3D sound that plays at maximum volume between 0 and 2 world units and attenuates at a distance of nearly 25 world units from the 3D sound's source position. The sound is also assigned to the same channel as $SimAudioType (Channel 2), so it will be affected by changes to that channel.

AudioProfiles (APs)

The AudioProfile datablock defines the sound that will be played. The AP tells the computer what sound file will actually be used for the sound. It also answers the question of whether the sound file should be preloaded. Preloading sounds helps when certain sounds would take too long to load in real time. The AP links itself to one AudioDescription (AD).

The following is an example of an AudioProfile:

```
datablock AudioProfile ( YourGameExplosionSound ) {
filename = "~/data/GPGTBase/sound/GenericExplosionSound.ogg";
```

```
description = YourGameNonLooping3DADDB;
};
```

Once again using the datablock keyword, this creates an instance of AudioProfile named YourGameExplosionSound to be used for a big fireball explosion noise. It is set to the file GenericExplosionSound.ogg and uses our non-looping 3D sound set in our previous example of an AudioDescription.

New and Datablock Keywords

You may notice that sometimes new AudioDescriptions and AudioProfiles (AD/APs) set themselves using datablock keywords, while others use the keyword new. The difference between the two is significant, so don't make the mistake of thinking that the usage of new or datablock can be done arbitrarily.

Objects created with the new keyword are not networkable, which means that they cannot be played by remote clients (a factor that is essential if you are creating a multiplayer online game). Objects that use the datablock keyword are absolutely networkable and can be used in online games. So consider whether your game will go online before using new or datablock to create sounds.

Engineering Sounds in Torque

We're going to look at creating static in-game sound effects and environmental sound effects. Some of this will use programming AD/AP code, but it will all enhance the immersive believability of the game environment.

In-Game SFX

There's some code in your game to make your player character tromp around. In other words, there are custom footsteps to the character's movements. Use a text editor to open YournameDemo\ server\scripts\player.cs, and near the top, just under all the $PlayerDeathAnim definitions, you'll see the start to Player Audio Profiles.

Each of these datablocks sets up an Audio Profile for a sound the player character might make. The first two are DeathCry and PainCry, or more obviously what sounds the character makes when it's dying and when it's hurt. The datablocks after that set up different SFX for footsteps, including the following plus more:

```
FootSoftSound = FootLightSoftSound;
FootHardSound = FootLightHardSound;
```

```
FootMetalSound = FootLightMetalSound;
FootSnowSound = FootLightSnowSound;
FootShallowSound = FootLightShallowSplashSound;
FootWadingSound = FootLightWadingSound;
FootUnderwaterSound = FootLightUnderwaterSound;
```

The creators of Torque intentionally used dummy digital audio files for every sound effect. Some of them sound pretty good, and you could leave them alone if you like. Or you can record your own digital sound files using Audacity or use footfall.wav in the projects\churchyard\sound folder on the CD. You must make sure you put the audio files you want to use in the YournameDemo\data\sound directory. You can replace the digital sound files with whatever digital sound files you like, as long as you write them correctly in your player.cs file in the datablocks. For instance, you might take this datablock:

```
datablock AudioProfile(FootLightSoftSound)
{
  filename = "~/data/sound/lgtstep_mono_01.ogg";
  description = AudioClosest3d;
  preload = true;
};
```

And you might change the file name to one of your own making:

```
datablock AudioProfile(FootLightSoftSound)
{
  filename = "~/data/sound/footfall.wav";
  description = AudioClosest3d;
  preload = true;
};
```

Save player.cs, delete the existing player.cs.dso file, and launch your game to try out your new walk sounds.

You can record different footstep sounds for when the player is walking over metal, under water, through shallow wading pools, over snow, and more, giving the player a special aural experience for each, as in Figure 9.4.

Using AudioEmitters

APs are one way to create sounds, but say that we want to have an environmental sound, such as the hooting of owls and creaking of crickets on a wind-swept hill or the roaring of waves and chirping of tropical birds. A completely dead silent

Figure 9.4
You can record sounds for every type of terrain the player crosses (*Zelda: The Twilight Princess,* images courtesy of Nintendo, 2007).

world is a dull and boring one. We're going to place a 3D sound into your game environment.

From the CD, copy the file projects\churchyard\sound\bg_noise.wav to YournameDemo\data\sound. Launch YournameDemo and go to the World Editor Creator. In the list, find Mission Objects, Environment, AudioEmitter, and click on AudioEmitter. In the pop-up window, click on OK. The AudioEmitter, by default, will appear in the center of the area onscreen that you are facing, so be sure you are looking in the direction where you want the sound to be heard before you add the AudioEmitter.

An AudioEmitter marker will be plunked down in the game level at the center of your screen, close to ground-level (see Figure 9.5). Press F11. The AudioEmitter has two spheres surrounding it. The inner sphere represents the minimum distance to hear the sound and the outer sphere represents the maximum distance to

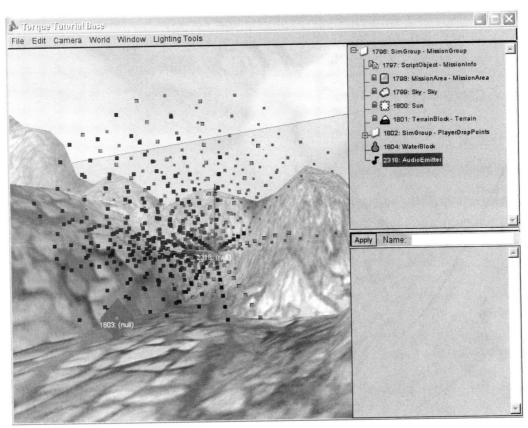

Figure 9.5
A 3D game sound is set by an AudioEmitter marker.

hear the sound. Typically, the larger the inner sphere, the farther sound will carry. Press F3 to go into the World Editor Inspector, and, with the marker selected, you'll see all its attributes appear in the lower-right panel for your editing pleasure. If you don't at first see the attributes show up, click on the emitter's gizmo.

Scroll through the attributes until you find Media > fileName, which should appear as a 0 because we haven't attached a sound file yet. Click on the browse button and choose bg_noise.wav. Make sure your speakers or headphones are on because you should hear the sound whenever you move closer to the swirling dots.

Hit Apply and save before you exit. Go back into your game and walk closer to the area where you remember placing the sound. With your speakers or headphones on and your volume up, you'll hear some interesting environment noise.

You can use this method to create sound effects for different areas of your game levels. You can have seabirds squawking just off the shore, farm animals near the village homes, and anything else that your imagination can come up with.

Review

At the end of this chapter, you should know the following:

- How sound has been used in TV and film to support narrative.

- What the difference is between "real" and hyper-real sounds.

- What all that sound engineer jargon about Hertz and decibels is all about.

- What influences sound effects, such as space, time, and events.

- How to soundproof and set up your own recording studio.

- What to remember when recording yourself.

- What the differences are between compressed and uncompressed file types.

- How to use Audacity to record, edit, and export audio files.

- How to use Torque to plug in your own custom sound effects.

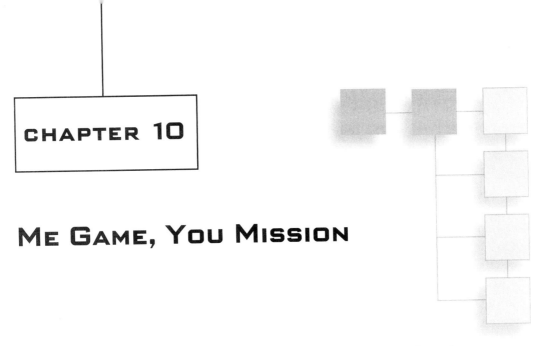

CHAPTER 10

ME GAME, YOU MISSION

Programming happens to be a two-way street. You must convince the computer to do what you want it to, while the computer has to interpret your commands and spit out what it thinks you want. Programming languages are tough to learn, but scripting languages, such as our TorqueScript, are a little easier. Scripting uses pre-existing engine elements to accomplish new tasks quickly and efficiently. You might wonder if it's truly necessary to code with TorqueScript, since Torque was actually written in C++ and assembly language, but if you don't know how to write in C++ from scratch, the scripting language will be easier.

In this chapter, we'll look at ironing out your game with scripting your mission. To do this, you must understand the mystic intricacies of TorqueScript.

Programming for Torque

Melv May is well known in the GarageGames community for his contributions to the Torque Demo and his fx-Improvements. The following are just a few of Melv May's tips to early indie developers:

- **"Prototype, Prototype, Prototype!"**—Do mock-ups, sketches, and preliminary game prototyping very early on. Don't wait or struggle to make one little thing "perfect" because you'll get way behind.

- **"Game or Demo?"**—Script what you're making and make sure you know what you're making. Is it a full-fledged game or just a brief technical demonstration of what you can do?

- **"Keep Alive"**—If you're working with a game design team, make sure to keep everyone informed of what you are doing at all times, no matter how irrelevant you think it is. The worst thing that can happen is that you make a bunch of changes to the code and then someone else says, "Nah, we didn't want to do that."

- **"Dark Period"**—Be prepared for disappointments and bleak periods during programming. Every designer wants to shoot himself in the foot or scrap the game and do something completely different once in a while. Be strong and carry on.

You don't have to be a total computer geek to make a great game. Sure, programming can seem monstrous to you at first, especially if you never quite took a shine to your math or science classes in school, but it can also be very rewarding to see your game come alive onscreen for the first time.

TorqueScript

TorqueScript should look familiar to you if you've ever done any programming before in the C/C++ languages. Most of the syntax is the same. A game script is composed of statements, object definitions, function declarations, and packages. Here are just a few of the most prominent features of TorqueScript that you should memorize:

- **Case sensitivity**—Variables and functions don't have to be proper case to work. For instance, %Aargh and %aargh would be read the same.

- **Ending statements**—Each and every statement must be concluded by a semicolon. This tells the script to close.

- **Ending algorithms**—A block that begins with an opening curly brace ({) must end with a closing brace (}) following the final statement.

- **Inheritance**—Torque allows you to expand on or override statements within the same script.

- **Variables**—The percent (%) sign before a name signifies that it is a local variable (an invented placeholder currently used within one function). The dollar ($) sign signifies that it is a global variable (a permanent placeholder). You can use alphanumeric characters (A-Z, a-z, 0-9) and the underscore character (_), but you can't start a variable name with a number.

- **Strings**—Constants enclosed in quotation marks are quite often used for in-game messages.

- **Echo**—The `echo()` command prints the value contained in a variable; for example, `echo ( "Hello world!" );` will have the words `Hello World!` pop up onscreen.

- **Booleans**—Torque uses Boolean variables, which can have only two values, like true or false.

- **Objects**—Definitions of objects come as a collection of attributes and behaviors.

- **Datablocks**—According to the Torque documentation, "Datablocks are special objects that are used to transmit static data from server to client," and they are used for the creation of most objects, from spawning monsters to playing music in the background.

- **Functions**—The basic algorithm you'll see in TorqueScript is a function, which starts, naturally, with the word `function`. If you define a function and then later on define a function with the same name, you'll be overriding the old function completely.

- **Packages**—You can place more than one function into a package, which starts with the word `package` and can be activated with `ActivatePackage()` and deactivated by `DeactivatePackage()`.

- **Classes**—No, this doesn't mean that you have to have any class to create games with Torque. Classes hang the level hierarchy for your game elements, and the core classes include `SimObject`, `SimDataBlock`, `SceneObject`, and `GameBase/GameBaseData`.

Al-Go-Rhythm

The best way to remember algorithm, because it's kind of a strange word, is "al-go-rhythm." An algorithm is a set of instructions, listed out step by step, to your computer. Your computer thinks in binary, or 1s and 0s (see Figure 10.1), and so you have to slow down and remember to "dumb down" your speech in order to communicate with your computer effectively. You don't literally have to

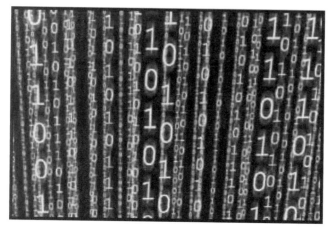

Figure 10.1
The true Matrix comes in binary (machine) code.

talk in 1s and 0s anymore (thank goodness!), but you do have to think logically, critically, and simply.

Most algorithms you'll write in TorqueScript appear as functions. They follow, statement by statement, until you reach the end of a function, and each function builds off descriptions and other functions. Some algorithms are pretty straightforward, while some others branch or loop back around. Usually, you can tell if an algorithm is set to loop if there's a return(); in it somewhere, and you can tell if an algorithm is branching if it has a conditional in it.

Conditionals are if-then/else statements. They're good for checking active variables. You check if a value is true, and if so you tell the machine to execute a function. If it's not true, it does not execute the function. Here's an example of a conditional statement in Torque:

```
if (%val)
 $firstPerson = !$firstPerson;
 ServerConnection.setFirstPerson ($firstPerson);
}
```

You could use if-then/else statements for lots of game-related items. For instance, you could check to see if the player's health bar is nil, and if so, call a function where his character dies. You could check to see if the player is out of ammo, and if so play an "empty" sound byte instead of gunfire. You could check to see if the player has wandered within the field of vision of a monster, and if so have the monster pounce on the player.

Perhaps the hardest thing for a new game designer to learn is programming, and most of it is learning to think like a machine. (The other part is just learning the syntax because the syntax is comparative to learning a second language.) Just remember, practice makes perfect.

Under the Hood of TorqueScript

First I want to show you how to add more fun stuff to your game. After that, you can experiment and come up with all kinds of other game programs.

Adding Score Items

So far your game opens up and simulates a client-server system. You can move your character around and explore the environment you've created. That's about it. We're going to add true functionality to the game.

Creating the Items

Copy the skull.dts file from the CD projects\churchyard\3d and paste it to a new folder called YournameDemo\data\shapes\skulls. This is the 3D model that you're going to use for the game so that Little Reaper can run around and find skulls like macabre Easter eggs. The skulls will serve the same purpose as the gold coins Mario picks up in the Nintendo games.

Now open YournameDemo\server\scripts\crossbow.cs in your text editor, scroll until you find the ItemData (Crossbow) datablock and insert the following code after the closing brackets of that datablock and before the next one starts. Remember to type clearly and consistently. Watch out because a typo can actually cause an error in your game or even hose your computer. When you type a code snippet like the ones I show you in this book, it is recommended that you stop and re-read what you've typed and compare it to what you were supposed to type so that you know you didn't miss anything.

```
datablock ItemData(Skull)
{
    // Mission editor category
    category = "Skulls";

    // Basic Item properties
    shapeFile = "~/data/shapes/skulls/skull.dts";
};
```

What this datablock does is tell the engine what your skull is and how to handle its usage. Datablocks contain information about the objects in your game. They're useful in networking because a datablock allows all the unchanging info about your objects to be sent across the network only once, whenever the client loads a new game.

Find and bring the skull into the Torque Editor. Go to World Editor Creator (F4) and, in the Shapes expanded list, you should see a roll-out list for Skulls. Click on Skull to drop the skull item onto your map; by default it should appear wherever your camera is currently facing. You can manipulate and move the skull around just like you did the crate in Chapter 6. Bring in 10 skulls, as this should be sufficient. Place them all around the Ravenscroft island and inside the church that you built. You're effectively hiding Easter eggs, so this should be a fun activity.

When you're done, go to Window > World Editor Creator and expand your MissionGroup. At the bottom of the list, you can see those skulls. Torque allows you to organize your skulls into a SimGroup, or folder, for easier management. To create a SimGroup, find the Mission Objects > System in the Creator Window. You'll see SimGroup. Go ahead and click on it. A dialog box will pop up asking for a new name for your SimGroup. Call it **Skulls** and click OK. Now, in the tree list, drag each of your skull shapes into the new skulls SimGroup (see Figure 10.2).

Scripting the Items

What you've just done is set up a datablock for Skull, a placeholder for the item that will give the player bonus points when Little Reaper touches it in the game world. Skull has a simple datablock containing only a couple of important data:

- Category tells the Mission Editor Creator what type of object it is.

- ShapeFile tells the engine where to find the data file for the actual shape of the object.

Skull by itself doesn't do too much, but now we're going to add real power to our Skull. Enter the following at the very bottom of the YournameDemo\server\ scripts\crossbow.cs file:

```
function Skull::onCollision(%this, %obj, %col)
{
   if(%col.getClassName() $= "Player")
   {
```

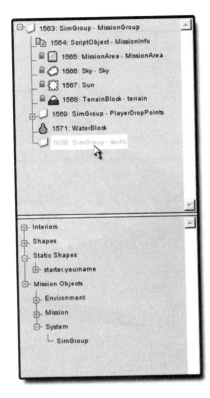

Figure 10.2
Creating the skulls SimGroup.

```
    %client = %col.client;
    %client.score++;
    commandToClient(%client, 'SetScoreCounter', %client.score);
    %obj.delete();
    %skullCount = Skulls.getCount();
    if(%skullCount > 0)
    return;
    // otherwise display victory screen
    commandToClient(%client, 'ShowVictory', %client.score);
    }
}
```

The onCollision function automatically activates when one object collides with another and causes the object to act more like a solid object. The engine must have three data elements in onCollision:

- **%this**—The datablock

- **%obj**—the individual object

- **%col**—the object that has been collided with

This line makes sure our skull has collided with the player's character:

```
if(%col.getClassName() $= "Player")
```

This defines %client as the client who touched the skull, then increments that client's score and sends a message to that client:

```
%client = %col.client;
%client.score++;
commandToClient(%client, 'SetScoreCounter', %client.score);
```

The following removes the skull and checks our Skulls SimGroup to see how many skulls still remain. If there are any skulls left, the script keeps waiting. If not, then a message goes out to the client telling him that victory has been achieved:

```
%obj.delete();
%skullCount = Skulls.getCount();
if(%skullCount > 0)
return;
// otherwise display victory screen
commandToClient(%client, 'ShowVictory', %client.score);
```

Save the script file and get ready because we're going to create a new one from scratch. Open up the YournameDemo\client\scripts folder and right-click in it to create a new text file that you will call clientMsg.cs. Open it up and type the following text:

```
function clientCmdSetScoreCounter(%score)
  {
  ScoreCounter.setText("Score:" SPC %score);
  }


function clientCmdShowVictory(%score)
  {
  MessageBoxYesNo("You found all the skulls!",
  "You want to play again?",
  "loadMyMission();",
  "quit();");
  }
```

Remember, back in Chapter 8, "Getting Gooey," you created the function for loadMyMission so that it would open up your game level. What you're doing here is letting the player jump back to the start of that game level if she wants to play again or exit Torque completely if she doesn't. Save and exit clientMsg.cs. You have to make sure that clientMsg.cs will be loaded correctly, so open Yourname Demo\client\init.cs and find the initializing client scripts section. At the bottom of the list—right under `exec("./scripts/centerPrint.cs");`—add the following (this will load your new script file when a new game loads):

```
exec("./scripts/clientMsg.cs");
```

Now when you go back to launch your game and start the World Editor (F11), you can select each of the skull objects, and, under their attributes, you'll find the Datablock field; this is where you should set the datablock for the skulls to say Skull. This should already be done for you, but if it is not, type **Skull** into that field or click on the browse button to the right and find where it says Skull. Save your mission and try it out. Little Reaper should run around and grab skulls. Once all 10 skulls are picked up, you should see the following message appear: "You found all the skulls!"

Work to Do

There are several more things that you can do at this point. For starters, you can take full advantage of the suite of materials already composed for you in the FPS Starter Kit, including weapons, ammo, health packs, AI, and more. You can start by editing or replacing the health bar, the crossbow, the ammo for the crossbow, and the health pack models. You can record your own sound effects for ambience and player actions and overwrite existing ones.

You can also go to www.garagegames.com and use the forums and questions section to find more code snippets and guides to add more usability to your game, like setting up characters to climb ladders, opening and shutting doors, particle effects you might not have thought of before, and much more. Another tip to encourage you, if you've discovered you have a knack for programming, is to pick up Kenneth C. Finney's book *3D Game Programming All in One* (see Figure 10.3), published by Premier Press in 2004. Written by a professional programmer who specializes in coding for Torque, this book and its successor, *Advanced 3D Programming All in One* (also by Finney; Thomson Course Technology, 2005), should provide you with extra tips and tricks.

Warning: watch out for feature creep! It's fine to add a few original features to your game, but the more you try to cram into one game design, the uglier the game will end up. Try to keep your overall design smooth and simple. Perfect a few features, and leave the rest out.

Figure 10.3
3D Game Programming All in One by Kenneth C. Finney.

It's not even imperative that you know TorqueScript inside and out. If you have the money and ingenuity, you can go online to www.rentacoder.com, where you will find several TorqueScript programmers looking for work. Each programmer is rated for your convenience. You post the work that you need completed, and programmers will supply you with bids. What is imperative is that you have a rudimentary understanding of computer logic and a clear plan for your game.

A good example of clear planning is in Hothead Games' upcoming serial MMO Penny Arcade Adventures, which starts with *Episode One: On the Rain-Slick Precipice of Darkness* (see Figure 10.4). With the clear visionary plan of Ron

Figure 10.4
On the Rain-Slick Precipice of Darkness (image courtesy of Hothead Games, 2007).

Gilbert, the team at Penny Arcade, and the developers at Hothead Games, this game is sure to catch on and be the best multiplayer online game of its kind. We'll talk about developing multiplayer games in the next chapter.

Review

In this chapter, you should have learned the following:

- How to program games for Torque using TorqueScript.

- What an algorithm is and the other keywords used in making one.

- How to load your new mission.

- How to add objects, script datablocks, and apply datablocks to objects in Torque.

- Where to go to find more ideas for scripting features in Torque.

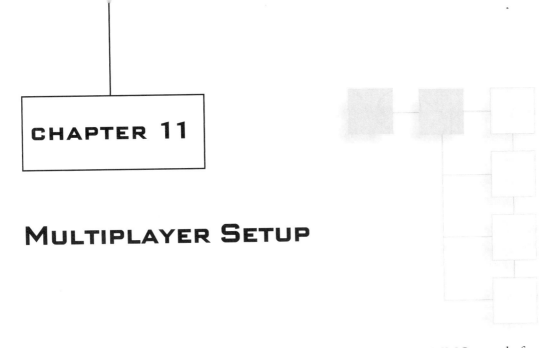

CHAPTER 11

MULTIPLAYER SETUP

MMO. It sounds like a health plan or insurance program. But MMO stands for massive multiplayer online game. The root of these online games came from MMORPGs, or massive multiplayer online role-playing games. MMORPGs, in turn, got started in the early days of the Internet as MUDs, or multi-user dungeons, which were text-based role-playing games based on the 1970s and 1980s Dungeons and Dragons games from TSR.

Today, the hottest online games are still role-playing games because RPGs lend themselves so well to the well-trod genre trends of hack 'n' slash loot-gathering, although there are several action games, especially armed forces squad-oriented ones. Plus, most of the next-gen console games have optional multiplayer campaigns built right in. Players who used to be stuck on their couches at home are now reaching out to insult other players via the Internet; and with broadband, DSL, and cable making hook-ups less expensive and more available, even more players are reaching out.

Designing the Next Big MMO

Tip

"Cost is the number one issue of MMORPG development. This is where we are going to see the MMORPG market begin to bifurcate along two lines."

—Jack Emmert, Cryptic Studios

Figure 11.1
World of Warcraft (image courtesy of Blizzard Entertainment, 2007).

The tip from Jack Emmert is from a recent article of his where he faces the upcoming crisis in MMO development. Too many publishers are afraid to come near multiplayer game proposals because they immediately compare them to *World of Warcraft* (see Figure 11.1). *WOW* did what few other games could do. Where *EverQuest* and *Dark Age of Camelot* had an audience subscription base of over 200,000 players, *WOW* had over one million. It is (at the time of this writing) the top-grossing MMORPG in the industry, with lots of competitors.

What most publishers don't realize is that *WOW* was so great at the time because Blizzard reportedly sunk between 50 and 70 million dollars into the project. Publishers may turn away game proposals that they worry won't turn out the number of sales *WOW* did, but they're not willing to handle the costs or admit that the investment proved the return.

In the end, a lot of MMO developers are turning to indie development and new economic models that are more efficient to get their games out there, even if

200,000 people don't sign up for any of them. These are MMOs that don't try to compete with *WOW* status. They'll hit their own niche markets.

Torque offers the indie developer everything he could ask for in MMO creation and maintenance.

TorqueNet

First of all, Torque uses the TorqueNet on all projects. The `loadMyMission` function sets up a simulated server and starts a new game. The reason we use a simulated server even in a single player game is because networking is so integral to the architecture of the Torque Game Engine. A network is simulated even when a game is going to be played solo or not on the Web. You may not have realized it, but even when you are building your game, your computer is simulating both a server and a client. You can even program login passwords and accounts, track player accounts, and ban people from your games. (These scripts are in the server folder, of course, if you feel like practicing with them.)

A *server* is the place where all your game world data is stored, and a *client* is an individual visitor that plays inside that game world. Think of it this way: A bowler goes into a bowling alley where he rents some shoes and takes his ball and starts bowling, and when he gets done he turns his shoes in and leaves with his ball. The bowling alley is the server and the bowler is a client.

There are essentially three connection schemes when you're setting up a multi-player networked game; the type of connection scheme that you use is obviously based on the type of game you are running.

- **Single player on single machine**—A single instance of the executable opens on a single machine and everything is run locally.

- **Active client and active server on single machine**—The one machine acts as a listen server. The hosting player, which would be you, uses a local client and a local connection, and other players use client-only executables, running on separate machines and connect remotely to the listen server. This is also known as hosting LAN (local-area network) parties.

- **Single executable running on dedicated server**—Your company hosts one or more sessions of the game on a machine you use as a dedicated server, and multiple client-only executables can connect to this server for multiplayer games.

Remote connections can be on a LAN or across the Internet; if you choose the Internet, a master server is required to host the game. The master server handles clients finding connections and ghost management.

Ghost Manager

TorqueNet features a Ghost Manager, which does two things: it "ghosts" objects from one host to the next, and it allows for information from the original object to pass to its ghosts. For example, imagine that you are playing a fantasy online game as a remote client. You round the top of the hill and see a tree standing there with a guardian under it. The tree and the guardian are not really on your end; they appear from the server and are ghosted to your machine so that you can see them. If the guard decides to attack you, Ghost Manager makes sure that there is very little lag time and that you see him attacking before he gets to your position. Ghost Manager allows for updates so that ghosts remain persistent to the original object.

Taking Your Game to the Next Level

I'm not going to get into networking and setting up a dedicated server, but I am going to make some suggestions.

First, you need to practice making solo player games on a single machine before launching into the complicated setup necessary for a multiplayer game. Don't just stick with *Abandon All Hope,* the game that you have made in this book. Make lots of different games of different genres, and try out your own missions and scripts until you have your own unique game style. Advertise yourself and your games online. Have your games available for download and get feedback from your players. If you have bugs in your games or consistent negative criticism, make changes in the way you design games to fix these bugs or get around the faults that people find in your work. Build yourself up as an awesome game developer and let the world know.

Once you are sure you can make great games, you can address making multiplayer games. Pick your favorite game that you've made. What are the core goals in it, and what is the storyline? Are there ways you can tweak these elements to make the game open to more than one player? Would the game work on a LAN or online? How many players would you want to have access to the game? With concrete answers to these questions, you can build the foundation for your multiplayer game.

Figure 11.2
A NetServ server and workstation from Prime Array Systems, Inc.

The unfortunate part of making a multiplayer game is that you will probably have to invest in more hardware (see Figure 11.2), including a second machine or a dedicated server or cabling. This list can get quite expensive; therefore, it is not recommended for beginners to leap in feet-first. Start small, and if things turn out well for you, take the steps to expand into the multiplayer market.

The MMO Workshop

Many of the code tricks that you will need to make a successful MMO have already been tried and proven in *Minions of Mirth* made by Prairie Games (see Figure 11.3). Prairie Games, as mentioned in Chapter 2, "The Torque Game Engine," have released the MMO Workshop, or Torque MMO Kit, which you can read more about online at www.mmoworkshop.com/trac/mom/wiki/FAQ. It is highly suggested that, if you are not an accomplished programmer or even if you are but you want to speed up your development schedule, you should try the Torque MMO Kit to build your online games.

Figure 11.3
Map of the world in *Minions of Mirth* (image courtesy of Prairie Games, 2005).

Review

You should have learned the following from this chapter:

- That big-time publishers often have big-time expectations of MMOs.

- That indie publishing is a great way to get your MMO out there.

- That Torque has built-in systems for MMO development, including TorqueNet and Ghost Manager.

- That MMO development can be quite costly, and thus you should start small and work up.

- That Prairie Games' MMO Workshop is a big boost to developing Torque MMO games.

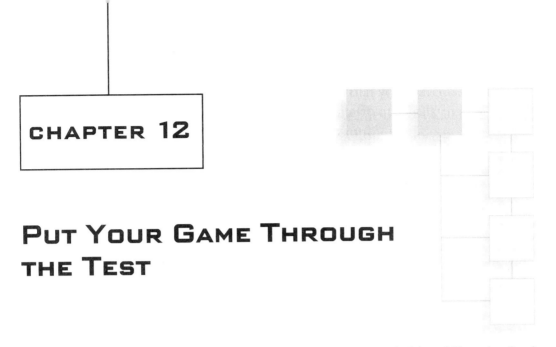

CHAPTER 12

Put Your Game Through the Test

This is it. You've created your first game, and you're probably adding the final touches. You have essentially reached the end of major production, but there is still so much more to do. First, you have to thoroughly test your game. Then, you have to advertise yourself and your game so that people know you exist. Once you establish a name for yourself (or preferably before), you can start making more games. In this chapter, I'll guide you through the testing stage.

Bug Testing

The testing of games for bugs, or erroneous glitches, has been developed into a fine art over the years. There are two reasons for this. One reason is that bug fixing can be time-consuming, and if it is simplified and made more efficient, then it can be over with more quickly. The other reason is that most companies can afford to hire multiple testers, called *beta testers,* and do research panels for quality assurance as well as testing for errors; with so many people brought in to work on a single project, it is in the company's best interests to have a clear and concise plan of attack when it comes to defending their game from bugs.

Reporting Bugs

An expedient method of bug testing is in paper reports (see Figure 12.1). When someone notices a bug that needs fixing, they write it down on paper. Beta testers

Figure 12.1
Reading the bug report.

have lots of paperwork to fill out, and bugs get categorized by their seriousness. The following list is a report of the separate classes of bugs:

- **A Class**—These bugs are major huge and get top priority; such glitches can be the computer screen freezing on loading, player characters dying during spawning, or vast tracts of virtual terrain suddenly disappearing.

- **B Class**—These bugs are still pretty major and should get some priority, but they are not so terrible that the tester cannot keep playing the game; such glitches include broken animation, erroneous messages, level leaks, bad guys not dying like they should, and more.

- **C Class**—These bugs are not major at all and sometimes get left in a game when it ships if the developers are being pushed toward a deadline by the publisher or feel pressured to "leave it"; such glitches can be NPCs not acting realistic, sound FX that are too loud, animation tics, and missing power-ups.

- **D Class**—There's usually not a real D Class for bugs. D Class is also called the "wish class" because these bugs are not glitches at all but what the tester sees as wrong in the game. Such problems can be choice of color palette, art style, voice direction, and storyline issues. Programmers may listen to criticism, but overall they don't worry themselves with D Class bugs.

Testers then spell out, word for word, exactly what the supposed glitch is, where it can be found, and, if the tester is knowledgeable enough, what they think is the cause of the concern. This way the development team can go back and track down the problem and attempt to fix it. Once the problem is assumed to be fixed, the team does not rest. A second testing will be done, and maybe even a third, until the fix has been verified and the bugs no longer exist.

Iterative Development

Of course, before the beta comes out and even before beta testers are pulled in, the development team of a game also runs through the same testing procedure on a regular basis to catch bugs before they even hatch; if you've followed the projects in this book, you've done the same, because there have been many times I've told you to implement a new section to the game or to the code and then test-run your game to make sure it works.

This is called *iterative development*, and it is important to verify your assets as you go. If you were to try to build an entire game from scratch, code it and put GUIs all over the place, before ever testing it out as you build, you may get a long string of errors and not know what you did to mess the game up. If you test each asset as you add it, you'll catch a mistake before you go on, and you can fix it immediately. If a feature doesn't work after multiple tries, then in all efficiency discard it and continue around it.

In all earnestness, you should stick to iterative development and test all of your assets as you build your game. Once you are through, show your game to a friend or two and have them play through the game to find the most obvious A and B Class bugs. If you have a game with multiple paths or multiple levels, you may have to get creative so that your testers can easily move from one area to the next and give the game a good thorough testing. This is where game developers usually design cheat codes.

You might've thought that cheat codes were programmed into games to be Easter eggs for gamers to find later on, right? You couldn't be further from the truth! Cheat codes are there so that the game's builders and testers can easily navigate through the entire game to do testing of all the game's assets. If a tester is looking for leaks in the levels, for instance, she is not going to be concerned about fighting enemies; so the God Mode is programmed into the game so that with a key combination the tester can make her character invincible while she wanders the levels looking for holes in the geometry.

Game developers used to just leave these cheat codes in when the game shipped because it was accepted practice for players to eventually learn these cheats. Today's developers are much more shrewd and delete the codes before distribution of the games because they figure that cheats shorten the lifespan of their games.

You can program your own cheat codes into your games using TorqueScript, if you like. However, just starting out you probably won't be making 50th-level games that are so confusing you need cheats to get around them, so don't sweat it.

Be Aware of the Top Issues

Following is a short checklist of the most important bugs to look for in your game as you go; there may be others, as this is an abbreviated list at best, and you can be sure that your harshest critics will discover them. But don't worry your head over anything that is not covered in this checklist.

- Does the game load okay? Does it freeze or open to the wrong area?

- Is the game interface clear enough that the player can get right into the game without getting lost or confused?

- Does the player's character appear? Can the player immediately tell where he is and what he's doing there? If he's in third-person mode, who is he?

- Do the spawning positions make sense given the strategy of the game?

- If the player is supposed to have a weapon, does the weapon appear where it's supposed to? Test it. Does it fire and reload as it should?

- If there are enemies, how close does the player have to get to them for them to react to the player? Is this reaction consistent and realistic? How much damage does the enemy do to the player? How much damage does the player do to the enemy? Is this consistent and realistic?

- Is the game indoors or outdoors? Are there any noticeable leaks in the level? Can the player character walk out of an area into blank space, for instance? Can the player see the edges of the world and realize that this is not real? Is there anything to take the player out of her suspension of disbelief?

- Is the scene properly lit so that plenty of detail can be seen without being washed out?

- Can the player character go where the designers want her to go without insurmountable obstacles in his way? Is the player character prohibited from going where he's supposed to, or is he "fenced in" correctly?

- Are the proportions of areas correct? Are doors and windows on buildings typical for the size of the player character and non-player characters? Are steps short enough so that the player character and non-player characters can walk up them?

- Does the player know what she is supposed to do in the game? Are there any ways that the player can get lost or confused about her mission? Is the main goal obvious? Does the storyline (if there is one) follow this goal consistently?

- Is the quality of the 3D modeling and 2D artwork up to par or the best that you can do? Are the art style, theme, and mood within the game consistent and well-coordinated? Is there anything that stands out as "not belonging"?

- Do all the player's run, strafe, jump, die, and root animations behave properly?

- Is there any time when the character seems to become invisible? This could point to a faulty LOD marker or mesh.

- Are the gameplay features easy to learn, understand, and use? Are there any features not consistent with the original game premise or the concept? Are there any features that feel like they don't belong?

Review

In this chapter you have learned the following:

- What bug testing is.

- How bug reports are done on paper and the different classes of bugs.

- The importance of rapid iterative development.

- What the top 10 issues are to be aware of.

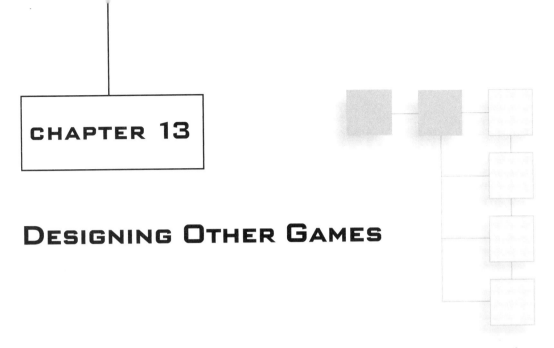

CHAPTER 13

DESIGNING OTHER GAMES

In this book, the majority of the projects have dealt with the FPS Starter Kit that comes shipped with the Torque Game Engine; and yeah, it makes for a really nice jump-off point for someone who wants to make a first-person or third-person game. But you might've noticed we didn't delve into the Racing Starter Kit, which also comes shipped with the engine, and we didn't discuss making other genre games. In fact, the Torque Game Engine is only the first step. There's also the Torque Game Builder, which helps you make 2D sprite-based platform games, and Torque X, which helps you make games for the Xbox 360. Let's take a short break before we continue to see just what your options are for making other games.

Games with the Torque Game Engine

Face it. You've already made one game with the Torque Game Engine. You've played with the Torque Editor and TorqueScript. You've made 3D models and DIF objects to go in your game. You've done a lot. Just because you've made one game with the Torque Game Engine doesn't mean you should stop there.

As several game gurus have pointed out in the past, typically your first three games (or more) will suck. It takes a while to get good at anything and that includes getting good at being a game designer. You should practice it if you want to get any better. Don't make just one game with the Torque Game Engine—make dozens! Get a feel for the Terrain Editor, the GUI Editor, and all the other little editors that have helped you to get this far. The easier game creation with this engine comes to you, the better you will get and the more you will truly express yourself in the game medium.

You could make more first-person and third-person shooter games with the FPS Starter Kit as a template. If you do so, choose a variety of fiction genres. Make a Western, a science-fiction game, a fantasy game, a modern thriller, or any combination in between. Experiment with plot and character and develop interesting and emotionally engaging stories. It might help you to re-read Freeman's emotioneering principles.

You could choose to take the Racing Starter Kit apart (shown in Figure 13.1). It's not that much different from the scripts and files associated with the FPS Starter Kit and just as easy to manipulate and make your own. You'll have more complex concerns, of course, when it comes to modeling a moving vehicle, but the concerns won't be so much different from the character carrying a firearm. You might also deign to add other characters to race against or simply make the race a timed challenge across even more unbelievably difficult terrain. It's really up to you.

Figure 13.1
The Torque Racing Starter Kit.

Games with Torque Game Builder

You can go online and download a trial version of TGB, the Torque Game Builder. 2D has a slightly different editor and set of rules than the 3D Torque Game Engine (as you can see in TGB's Animation Builder in Figure 13.2), but some of the design rules remain the same. You can create a clone of *Super Mario Bros.*, *Pac-Man*, *Space Invaders*, or any other retro sprite-based game. Of course, you can also leave conventions behind and make a truly unique and entertaining game about anything your imagination can dream up.

First, for those of you who don't know what a sprite is, it's an animated drawing that takes the place of characters, vehicles, and props in a flat or retro game. Sprites are drawn frame by frame and animated by cycling through their frames. Even the game *Donkey Kong Country*, which came out for the Super Nintendo, was still a sprite-based game, though the characters were modeled in 3D before being exported as flat images. See the sprite sheet in Figure 13.3.

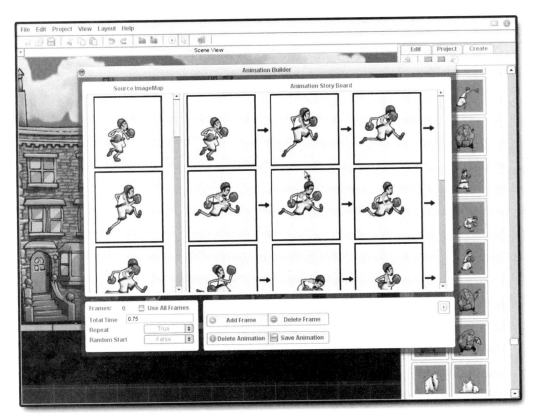

Figure 13.2
Animation Builder from the Torque Game Builder.

Figure 13.3
A sprite sheet from *Donkey Kong Country* (image courtesy of Nintendo, 1994).

One of the prime resources for sprites on the Net is the Spriters Resource (www.spriters-resource.com). Be aware that all its content is copyrighted by the original creators, however, so you can't make any money off using any pre-generated sprites you pull off there.

You might be asking yourself, "Why make retro games? Aren't they old-fashioned?" The answer is "Not at all!" Retro games are seeing a huge comeback right now. Part of the reason you see retro games gaining popularity again is because 3D video games are hitting an ideal plateau, where details and realism are competing with efficient and entertaining gameplay. A lot of game designers are going with more graphic realism, and so gameplay has begun to suffer. Games don't have to have terrific graphics to be fun, which is some-thing we've all known since the first *Zork* game came out (see Figure 13.4). Thus some developers are going back to the 2D sprite-based games and focusing more intently on perfecting gameplay, making games more fun to play.

Figure 13.4
The first *Zork* game (image courtesy of Sierra Online, 1977).

If you choose to, you can join the crowd by making your own sprite-based games with the Torque Game Builder. The scripting and the editors are more or less the same, with the exception that you are working on a flat canvas rather than a 360-degree virtual plane.

Games with Torque X

As stated in Chapter 2, "The Torque Game Engine," Torque X was released at the same time as the XNA as an alternative for game designers to create Microsoft Xbox Live Arcade games for the Xbox 360 (see the console in Figure 13.5). The only drawback, from the standpoint of finishing the projects in this book, is that Torque X uses the Torque Game Builder and the C# programming language, which has some minor similarities to TorqueScript but is simply not the same.

Yet if you want to develop your own Xbox 360 games, you won't let that stop you. There are some basic tutorials and C# programming code snippets online that will help you. The same principles you've learned from this book will aid you in creating great games. You don't even have to purchase an XNA Creators Club membership if all you want to do is create video games for your personal

Figure 13.5
The Xbox 360 game console (image courtesy of Microsoft, 2007).

Xbox 360; you can use a cable connection to transfer your game to your console. But if you want to share your game online through the popular Microsoft Xbox Live Arcade, you must first have an XNA Creators Club membership (which at the time of this writing is less than $10 a month), and you must also create an Xbox Live Arcade account.

Torque X helps you take your games to the console market, which is a rare thing for such remarkable game engine software.

Final Thoughts

Your games can be about anything you want. You can make a game about a private detective solving crimes in the dark wharf town of a fantasy world, where orcs and goblins hold power as the local Mafia (see Figure 13.6). Or you can make a game about a vengeful cowboy who has to learn to use an alien blaster to defeat the outlaws that killed his family. Or you can make a game about a cute little witch girl who has to find all the ingredients to brew a love potion to make a warlock fall in love with her. The options are truly open ended with the only limitations being the extent of your imagination and your practiced skill with the game engine.

If you decide that there's one area of game design you prefer, find some team-mates who have preferences in the areas that you are weak in. Make great games

Figure 13.6
Fantasy and detective fiction genre.

together. Or if you decide that this is going to be your career goal, get through high school with good grades and jump into a college that teaches game design or game art. There are several, including the following, which you can find by searching at Google:

3D Training Institute

Academy of Art University

American Sentinel University

Collins College

Daniel Webster College

DeVry University

DigiPen Institute of Technology

Digital Media Arts College

Emagination Game Design

Ex'pression College for Digital Arts

Full Sail Real World Education

Global Institute of Technology

iD Tech Camps

International Academy of Design and Technology

ITT Technical Institute

Media Design School

Pacific Audio Visual Institute

Sanford-Brown College—St. Charles

Seneca College's Animation Arts Centre

The Academy of Game Entertainment Technology

The Art Institute and Art Institute Online

The Florida Interactive Entertainment Academy

The Game Institute

The Guildhall at SMU

The School of Communicating Arts

University of Advancing Technology

Vancouver Institute for Media Arts

Westwood College of Technology

Westwood Online College

You could also try to get a job with a major game company; many of them hire regular animation students who have no formal game design training, but who are skilled at modeling, texturing, lighting, or animation. Take a look at the global map of game companies online at www.gamedevmap.com.

The choices are up to you. In the next chapter, we will focus on promoting your garage games and getting people to play your homemade games.

Review

In this chapter, you have learned the following:

- How to make other games with the Torque Game Engine.

- Optional game design choices with the Torque Game Builder and Torque X.

- Formal game design schools you could choose from.

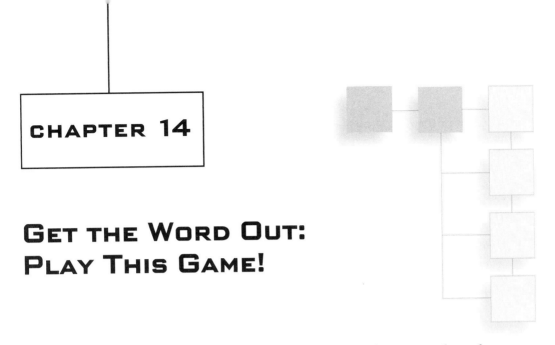

CHAPTER 14

GET THE WORD OUT: PLAY THIS GAME!

Eventually you're going to reach the end of your production cycle and want to advertise the homebrewed game you've made using Torque. When you get to that point, you may know a few friends you want to tell, but to really get the most people playing your game, you're going to have to be savvy. Or you might want to sell your game, which is a whole other animal. You might even want to take your game to a noted publisher and see if they'll run with it (a dream that can sometimes become a reality). Whatever you want to do to get the world to notice you and your game, I'll show you how in this chapter.

Developing a Proposal

If you have finished your game but feel you could do better with a bigger budget or a bigger team of developers, you should consider developing a game proposal and seeking out game publishers to back you.

When working on your game proposal, which is similar if not based on your game design document, keep in mind the difference between those materials intended for internal use and those you want a publisher to see. When writing game proposals, most companies do not include every detail. The most important details the publisher needs to understand are as follows:

- You know what you are doing and have the skills to pull off the project you propose.

- The game you propose looks good. Notice I said "looks." You can talk a good game, but until you have a demo (especially a playable prototype) to show a publisher, they usually won't give you the time of day.

- Your proposed game has all the earmarks of a bestselling game.

- You have set your company above all the rest by being fresh, innovative, and appealing. You have a clear identity and a great gimmick.

When you go before a publisher or design house, try to secure a face-to-face meeting with them to deliver and review your proposal. This way, you can elaborate on specific points that you think are important. You can also answer clarifying questions faster. Just remember to go in prepared, collected, and dressed nicely.

Your proposal can be on paper, but it is recommended you use visual media. You can use Microsoft PowerPoint to develop a slideshow presentation. You could set up a demo of the game right there or show them a pre-recorded demo of gameplay. You want the freedom to discuss and evolve your game description while also answering questions. In most cases, the publisher's willingness to listen will be directly related to the energy you impart, so go in pumped and excited about your own game. In most cases, if you're under the age of 18, a publisher will want to work with someone older as an intermediary, if they give you the time of day at all. Be forewarned that this is not an easy row to hoe; in fact, it's much easier to self-publish and self-promote your own games, which—as you saw in Chapter 1, "So You Want to Be a Game Designer?"—is an easy plan to choose in this cyber age of garage games.

Tooting Your Own Horn

Some guys and gals find it difficult to promote themselves. If you place yourself in this category, you're not alone. Even the sensational singing legend Madonna was prone to self-doubt, and she has been recognized the world over as one of the best self-promoters. You might be plagued by insecure feelings and doubts, or you might be really self-confident but feel selfish or that you have to be humble. Don't be! If you want people to notice you and play your game, you can't be a fly on the wall. You have to be just as crazy, outlandish, and noticeable as possible.

Now I'm not advocating that you dress like Marilyn Manson (as seen in Figure 14.1) when you stroll down the streets of your hometown. And if you plan to visit with a publisher or conduct yourself in a business atmosphere, you better wear a dress or a

Figure 14.1
Marilyn Manson addressing Temple University (image courtesy of Temple News, 2007).

tie. You're expected to dress the part of the environment you're entering; as the adage goes, "When in Rome, do as the Romans do." If you're hanging around a game design company where everyone's wearing T-shirts and blue jeans, then you'd better wear a T-shirt and blue jeans. But if you're going into a board room to negotiate contracts with your publisher, you'd best put on a dress or tie (whatever's acceptable for your gender and zip code).

What I am telling you to do is to stop being vague, colorless, wishy-washy, or the amazing invisible man or woman. People won't notice you if you don't want to be noticed, and that's a shame because you deserve to be noticed. Now you might be saying, "But it's my game that I want people to notice, not me," and that's true. But if you are an unnoticeable person used to evading comment and keeping to yourself, then there's a great possibility your game's never going to get noticed.

Have a Clear Identity

A lot of companies talk about using a gimmick. A gimmick is a clear image that represents an idea. A gimmick helps to sell products. You've noticed gimmicks all around you, and some of them can be very transparent or clumsy, but most often a gimmick is purely an understandable image of an idea that takes too long to explain. Think about your game idea. Can you express it in a single, clear sentence? Can you express it in a single image or avatar? If not, you might have to develop a gimmick to sell your game.

Taking time to write down your game (as discussed in Chapter 3, "Creating a Basic Game Outline") helps you to sharpen and clarify your game idea to yourself and to the team that you'll be working with. If you skipped doing this or made the game first before taking the time to simplify your concept, then you need to work it out right now, before going any further.

Once you've simplified your game idea, consider the following and find one thing that would serve as a possible gimmick:

- **Character**—Do you have a cute, sexy, strong, or mysterious character that is different enough and exciting enough to serve as an icon for your game?

- **Place**—Is the setting for your game adventurous, glorious, beautiful, or mysterious enough to serve as an icon for your game?

- **Weapon**—Does your character wield an interesting, powerful, cool, or different sort of weapon that looks neat enough to serve as an icon for your game?

- **Enemy**—Do you have a scary, awesome, powerful, or mysterious enemy that is enthralling enough to serve as an icon for your game?

- **Element**—Is there some gameplay element so infusive that it's found everywhere in your game and looks different and exciting enough to serve as an icon for your game?

Let me give you just a few examples of gimmicks other games have used, in case you're still confused. In *Tomb Raider*, the gimmick is Laura Croft, in *Super Mario Bros* it's Mario, in *Donkey Kong Country* it's Donkey Kong, and in *Zelda* it's the elf Link. All of these games have the main character as a gimmick. In *Prince of Persia: The Sands of Time*, the gimmick is a combination of the main character (the Prince) and the place (the romanticized Ancient Persia). In the games *Diablo* and *Rayman: Raving Rabbids*, the gimmicks are the enemies (see Figure 14.2).

You have to find just the right look for yourself, the right gimmick for your game, and you want people to notice you and play your game. Because you've worked hard at creating a fun game, which people will like, you will know you're not offering them empty promises. You are only giving them excellent entertainment.

Okay, but how do you get the world to notice you and your game? How do you clue folks in that you have something for them to play? One of the best ways in this beautiful cyber age is through online communities.

Figure 14.2
The Raving Rabbids of *Rayman: Raving Rabbids* (image courtesy of Ubisoft, 2006).

Online Communities

Online communities are Web sites designed to foster communication and net-working. They've been compared to bulletin boards, social clubs, and school-yards. They're somewhere you can go to chat and interact with "real-world" peers, as well as people you've never met before from all over the world. The World Wide Web, since its heralding by Tim Berners-Lee, has exploded with hundreds of community Web sites, many of them utterly vast in scope, such as MySpace, Friendster, Bebo, and Facebook.

Most social networks over the Internet are open to the public and anyone can join, although each individual site has its own User Agreement, which may have specific rules or regulations joiners have to follow. Most of these networks are free to join, which is one of the reasons they've become so popular. Sites like MySpace are exclusively funded by all the advertising taking up screen real estate. Another plus to these networks is you don't even have to use your real name; you can create unlimited alter egos or work from an anonymous entity.

What you get out of these sites is entirely up to you, of course. But as we are discussing the promotion of your games, that's one thing you can achieve on these sites. The Great Games Experiment, or GGE, hosted by the folks at GarageGames, is an online community whose sole purpose is for gamers to find games and game developers to share their games and game design advice; so GGE (see Figure 14.3) is one community you can join to promote your games to the world. You can find it online at www.greatgamesexperiment.com.

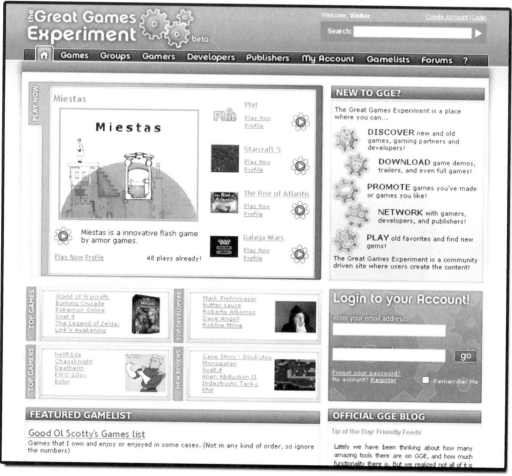

Figure 14.3
The Great Games Experiment.

Of course, with over 200,000 new accounts created each and every day and over 106 million users, MySpace is an even larger online community and a proven ground for sharing and experimentation. It could net you thousands of more players and friends. You are free to join as many online communities as you want and promote yourself and your games on any of them that allow it. But for now we'll focus on getting into MySpace.

Setting Up a MySpace Page

If you're some kind of Internet-savvy teenager, there's a chance you already have a MySpace page and belong to most of the online communities. If this is the case, feel free to skip this section entirely. You can begin promoting yourself right away by placing on your site pages some images from your game, some Desktop goodies, and playing a short trailer. Then invite all your online friends to try your games out and spread the word through chat. If you've never considered a community account before and don't even know what MySpace is, then you should read on.

Go to www.myspace.com and you should find yourself on a local MySpace site (as shown in Figure 14.4). Click the Sign Up button in the top-right corner of the

Figure 14.4
MySpace.com.

page and proceed to fill out the online form that appears. By default, your Profile page will only publicly display your first name, age, and location, so don't worry about your privacy at this time. You have to be 14 years or older to sign up for a MySpace account, however. MySpace has begun cracking down on underage account holders, so you might have to try Facebook or Friendster if you're younger than 14.

You need to have an active e-mail address or Web mail account. Your MySpace password has to be at least six characters long and contain both letters and numbers. After you click on Sign Up at the end of filling out this form, you'll be prompted to upload your first image, which will appear as your face on MySpace, unless you change it later. You can't submit anything offensive or rude or the copyrighted work of others. In fact, as a game designer, you should use your personal photo, a company logo (if you have one), or some art from your game. You can only upload a JPG or GIF, and it must be smaller than 600 KB in file size.

Next you'll assign your MySpace URL or name (they're the same thing). The URL, or uniform resource locator, is your Profile's address out there on the Web. Your URL at the start will begin (always) with http://www.myspace.com/ and will end in a ridiculous string of numbers. Click on the link and enter your desired moniker; it can be anything, as long as nobody else is using it, but keep in mind that it should be short and descriptive.

You want people to associate you with the games that you build. For this, you're going to have to make an online personality. Keep in mind the image you want to portray and the gimmicks for your game that you've developed. To get started, click the Edit Profile option found in the list next to your image at the top of your Hello page. This opens the Profile Edit page. The page's tab reveals the numerous sets of fields where you can add personal details. You want to balance search-ability with privacy. In other words, you want people to find you, and you want them to know about the games you've made, but at the same time you don't want them knowing too much about you because some people can't be trusted.

The most important field here is the one that says About Me. Tell the whole world who you are and what games you make, and you can write it however you like. You might want to pre-write this text copy in Microsoft Word first, spell-check it, or even run it by your friends or parents, before you add it to your MySpace page. This will develop people's first impression of you, so you want it to matter. Last but not least, under the Name tab, find Display Name and make sure your moniker here reflects who you are or what you do.

You might want to blog, too. You could type entries online covering the development cycle you have going of upcoming games; this is known as keeping a development journal online. Or you could write updates of when a new game is coming out or post bug reports. Whatever you can think of to type for a blog, you can do it from your MySpace account. Enter your Blog Control Center and click on Customize Blog in the My Controls box. A page will come up with a long list of tabs and fields, each controlling different page elements and customizing the look of your blog. You can read more about the blog on www.myspaceblogr.com.

To get started, log in to MySpace and click Blog on the MySpace navigation bar, then click Post New Blog within the My Controls panel on the left. Just like e-mail, blogs have two parts: a subject and a body. The subject is just like a headline, while the body's where your real text should go.

There's a community in MySpace for games, although usually it's for gamers looking for games. This is a great place to tap in and make friends. However, besides short Flash games and files with relatively short file sizes, you cannot upload your Torque games to MySpace. You'll have to get your file hosted somewhere else, and then post a link to your game downloads in your blog or directly on your Profile page (and anywhere else you want to, as well). The following are some places you can host your files:

- Files Upload (www.files-upload.com)

- Wiki Upload (www.wikiupload.com)

- MyDataBus (www.mydatabus.com)

What's Next?

The sky's the limit! You now have the beginnings of becoming a great game designer. You know what to do, but especially what not to do. You know how to put together a first-person or third-person video game using the Torque Game Engine. You know how to let the world know you and that your games exist and how to find players for your games.

The next step is up to you. Are you going to sit on the couch and play games? Or are you ready to take it to the next level and sit in front of your computer and make awesome games all your own? You have to make that decision. What's it going to be?

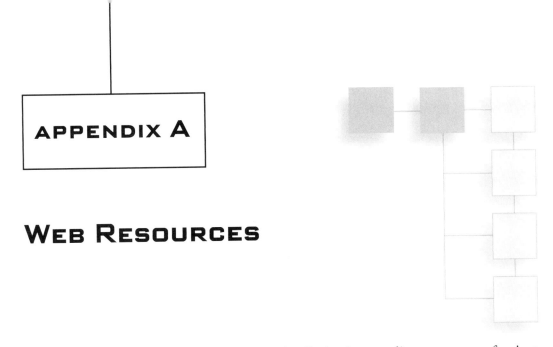

APPENDIX A

Web Resources

This appendix should provide you with all the best online resources for just starting out with the Torque Game Engine and your newfound place as a game designer. This list is by no means a complete one. If you wish to find more resources, simple use an Internet search engine, such as Google, and type in the keywords you're searching for, such as "free sound effects" or "dts models"— and you'll be surprised what you can find on your own.

Links

The following links are divided into separate headings for your ease of finding the Web address you need.

Torque Related

The following are Web addresses for places with information specific about the Torque Game Engine or the creators of Torque, GarageGames.

Home page for GarageGames, maker of Torque:
www.garagegames.com

Content Packs, pre-made content to supercharge your games:
www.garagegames.com/developer/torque/contentpacks/

Torsion TorqueScript IDE, a script editor by Sickhead Games:
www.sickheadgames.com/

The Official Torque Documentation and User's Guide:
www.garagegames.com/docs/tge/general/index.html

The Official Torque Game Engine SDK Documentation:
www.garagegames.com/docs/tge/

Torque Developer Network, reference site for Torque:
http://tdn.garagegames.com

Torque Developer Tool Store, professional game making tools at every level:
www.garagegames.com/makegames/

Great Games Experiment, promotion and network site for gamers and game developers:
www.greatgamesexperiment.com/

Help Wanted Ads, GarageGames' classifieds:
www.garagegames.com/index.php?sec=mg&mod=marketplace&page=jobs

Game Development in General

The following Web addresses are for information and networking among game developers.

GameMD, a kind of WebMD for game designers seeking help with their projects:
www.gamemd.net/

GamaSutra, the game design news and article site:
www.gamasutra.com/

GameDev.net, reference site for all game developers:
www.gamedev.net/

Freeman Group, Creating Emotions in Games:
www.freemangames.com/idea/

Articles by Greg Costikyan:
www.costik.com/writing.html

Manifesto Games, indie game network site:
www.manifestogames.com/

Art Resources

The following Web addresses are for artists seeking fonts, interface design, concept sketches, and free textures.

1001 Free Fonts, a resource site for artists:
www.1001freefonts.com/

GUIStuff.com, free GUI tutorials:
www.guistuff.com/tutorials.shtml

Linux Artist, a resource site for Linux OS artists:
www.linuxartist.org/

Turbo Squid, free 3D models and textures for game artists:
www.turbosquid.com/

Sound Resources

The following Web addresses are for free sound effects, music, and audio help when making games.

Amppisound, one-stop source for music and sound FX for games:
www.amppisound.com/

Shockwave-Sound, free music and sound loops:
www.shockwave-sound.com/

Ogg Vorbis, open-source audio encoding:
www.vorbis.com/

Contributor's Web Sites

Finally, I would like to acknowledge the contributors to this book; many of them have more helpful resources you can find on their Web sites or content you can purchase to make game creation for Torque easier.

Tridinaut, makers of 3D models for Torque games:
www.tridinaut.com/

Frogames, makers of uniquely styled DTS and DIF files specifically for Torque:
www.frogames.net/

Marino Sounds, creator Manuel Marino's site for sound FX and music for Torque games:
www.manuelmarino.com/

Prairie Games, Inc., makers of *Minions of Mirth* and the MMO Workshop/ Torque MMO Kit:
www.prairiegames.com/

Hothead Games, the developers of Penny Arcade Adventures:
www.hotheadgames.com/

Dark Horizons, developers of *Lore:*
www.darkhorizons-lore.com/

Mode7 Games, developers of the game *Determinance:*
www.mode7games.com/

BraveTree Productions, LLC, developers of *ThinkTanks:*
www.bravetree.com/

Chronic Logic, LLC, game developer/publisher of *Kingdom Elemental* and *Microwarrior:*
www.chroniclogic.com/

Pocketwatch Games, makers of *Wildlife Tycoon: Venture Africa:*
www.pocketwatchgames.com/

Waking Games, developers of *Once Upon a Time:*
www.wakinggames.com/

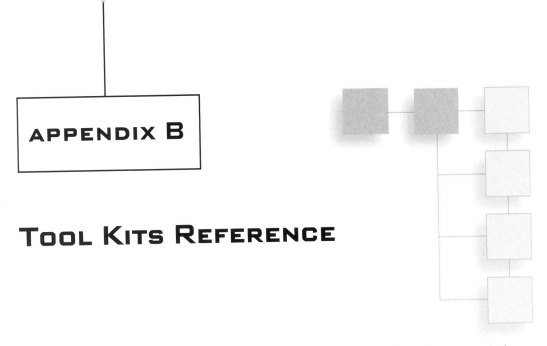

APPENDIX B

TOOL KITS REFERENCE

Everything that is located on the CD can be confusing at first glance, and if you are looking for something specific (for instance, if you are told in one of the projects in this book to find a target file and copy and paste it to your work folder), then this appendix is here to help you.

Companion CD-ROM Contents

Upon entering the CD, you should be able to navigate by the various file headings, and as such, you should find the files forthwith under their appropriate headings.

Demos

This folder includes trial versions of several games that have been created using the Torque Game Engine, such as the following:

- *Dark Horizons: Lore*—Now you can be in the mech-suit hot seat!

- *Determinance*—A sword-swinging action game.

- *Marble Blast Gold*—A fun puzzle game to make you lose your marbles.

- *Once Upon a Time*—A multiplayer action game set in a fairy-tale book.

- *Orbz*—Another great puzzle game.

- ***ThinkTanks***—Brains attached to tanks? What could go wrong?

- ***Warzone Demo***—An interactive demo of the power of the Torque Game Engine.

- ***Wildlife Tycoon: Venture Africa***—A real-time game with real game animals.

Software

This folder contains full and trial versions of software you will find helpful in creating games with Torque, including the following:

- **Audacity**—A free sound editing software.

- **Blender**—A free 3D modeling package based on Python.

- **Paint Dot Net**—A free paint program similar to Photoshop.

- **Torque Constructor**—A free DIF file making application.

- **Torque ShowTool Pro**—A free Torque game asset preview application.

- **Sickhead Games: Torsion**—A syntax editor for TorqueScript for PC users.

Projects

This folder has all the files needed (besides the ones you have to make yourself) for working through the projects in this book, including specifically

- **Chapter 5**   The bricks.jpg for creating your own custom texture.

- **Chapter 6**—The crate DIF file you make starting out with Torque Constructor.

- **Chapter 7**—The template files and textures you need for creating Little Reaper in 3ds Max.

- **Chapter 8**—The welcomeBG.jpg file for the interface background.

■ **Churchyard**—Miscellaneous files you'll need to create the *Abandon All Hope* game.

Resources

This folder shares with you the wonderful contributions by such authors as Frogames, Tridinaut, and Manuel Marino. There are DTS (model) files, DIF (interior) files, custom sounds, music, textures, and so much more inside.

Figures

This folder has all the original image files used in this volume for you to view on your computer. This can come in handy if the print resolution makes details difficult to see, or if you simply want to enjoy the pictures in full color.

INDEX

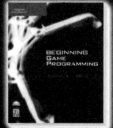

License Agreement/Notice of Limited Warranty

By opening the sealed disc container in this book, you agree to the following terms and conditions. If, upon reading the following license agreement and notice of limited warranty, you cannot agree to the terms and conditions set forth, return the unused book with unopened disc to the place where you purchased it for a refund.

License

The enclosed software is copyrighted by the copyright holder(s) indicated on the software disc. You are licensed to copy the software onto a single computer for use by a single user and to a backup disc. You may not reproduce, make copies, or distribute copies or rent or lease the software in whole or in part, except with written permission of the copyright holder(s). You may transfer the enclosed disc only together with this license, and only if you destroy all other copies of the software and the transferee agrees to the terms of the license. You may not decompile, reverse assemble, or reverse engineer the software.

Notice of Limited Warranty

The enclosed disc is warranted by Thomson Course Technology PTR to be free of physical defects in materials and workmanship for a period of sixty (60) days from end user's purchase of the book/disc combination. During the sixty-day term of the limited warranty, Thomson Course Technology PTR will provide a replacement disc upon the return of a defective disc.

Limited Liability

THE SOLE REMEDY FOR BREACH OF THIS LIMITED WARRANTY SHALL CONSIST ENTIRELY OF REPLACEMENT OF THE DEFECTIVE DISC. IN NO EVENT SHALL THOMSON COURSE TECHNOLOGY PTR OR THE AUTHOR BE LIABLE FOR ANY OTHER DAMAGES, INCLUDING LOSS OR CORRUPTION OF DATA, CHANGES IN THE FUNCTIONAL CHARACTERISTICS OF THE HARDWARE OR OPERATING SYSTEM, DELETERIOUS INTERACTION WITH OTHER SOFTWARE, OR ANY OTHER SPECIAL, INCIDENTAL, OR CONSEQUENTIAL DAMAGES THAT MAY ARISE, EVEN IF THOMSON COURSE TECHNOLOGY PTR AND/OR THE AUTHOR HAS PREVIOUSLY BEEN NOTIFIED THAT THE POSSIBILITY OF SUCH DAMAGES EXISTS.

Disclaimer of Warranties

THOMSON COURSE TECHNOLOGY PTR AND THE AUTHOR SPECIFICALLY DISCLAIM ANY AND ALL OTHER WARRANTIES, EITHER EXPRESS OR IMPLIED, INCLUDING WARRANTIES OF MERCHANTABILITY, SUITABILITY TO A PARTICULAR TASK OR PURPOSE, OR FREEDOM FROM ERRORS. SOME STATES DO NOT ALLOW FOR EXCLUSION OF IMPLIED WARRANTIES OR LIMITATION OF INCIDENTAL OR CONSEQUENTIAL DAMAGES, SO THESE LIMITATIONS MIGHT NOT APPLY TO YOU.

Other

This Agreement is governed by the laws of the State of Massachusetts without regard to choice of law principles. The United Convention of Contracts for the International Sale of Goods is specifically disclaimed. This Agreement constitutes the entire agreement between you and Thomson Course Technology PTR regarding use of the software.